12 Rules for Christian Activists

12 Rules for Christian Activists

A Toolkit for Massive Change

Ellen Loudon

CANTERBURY
PRESS

Norwich

© Ellen Loudon 2020

Published in 2020 by Canterbury Press
Editorial office
3rd Floor, Invicta House,
108–114 Golden Lane,
London EC1Y OTG, UK
www.canterburypress.co.uk

Canterbury Press is an imprint of Hymns Ancient & Modern Ltd
(a registered charity)

Hymns Ancient & Modern® is a registered trademark of
Hymns Ancient & Modern Ltd
13A Hellesdon Park Road, Norwich,
Norfolk NR6 5DR, UK

British Library Cataloguing in Publication data

A catalogue record for this book is available
from the British Library

978-1-78622-244-2

Typeset by Regent Typesetting
Printed and bound by
CPI Group (UK) Ltd

Contents

Contents

Acknowledgements

I am very grateful to everyone who has collaborated on this book and the generosity with which they have shared their practice and thinking. You are all remarkable Christian activists who are participating in massive change.

As well as those who have written contributions, there are many others who have spent time with me drinking tea, bouncing ideas about and offering encouragement. I am particularly grateful to Mark Loudon and Miranda Threlfall-Holmes, who have had my back and kept the pressure on. Also, thank you to members of the Tsedaqah community who have inspired and helped me – particularly Sam Rigby and Jen Williams for their research skills.

Thanks to David Shervington at Canterbury Press, who has kept the project on track, and Miranda Lever for her clarity and editing skills.

Finding time to write in the middle of the excitement of a full-time role in the Diocese and Cathedral of Liverpool has been a challenge only made possible because of the excellent colleagues with whom I share my working life. Together in the Diocese of Liverpool we are asking God for a 'bigger church to make a bigger difference, so that we see more people knowing Jesus and more justice in the world'. This book is a small contribution to this vision.

Foreword

It's a pleasure to work alongside Ellen Loudon in Liverpool and to learn from her about Jesus and justice. Now you too can share this pleasure by reading and absorbing her ideas, and those of her outstanding team of collaborators, in this book. You'll read stories of planning, diversity, courage, focus, prayer, passion, holiness, grace, sheer hard work – because all these and more add up to the life of a Christian activist.

Here in Liverpool Diocese we aim to be a community of people committed to Jesus and justice. We sense God's calling and sending in a twofold journey – the inner calling to pray, read and learn, and the outer sending to tell, serve and give. In these chapters, Ellen and her friends articulate in a whole range of different ways what all this might mean for those who are led to change the world by the grace and power of God.

But here at the beginning of the journey, let me warn you. If you decide to read further, look out! You will read about the need for massive change, and you will be asked to commit to massive change yourself. This is a book full of solidarity, lightness and joy – but it is very well aware of the strength needed to struggle for justice and humanity in the face of so much inequality, prejudice and hate. It will invite you, in the words of the American Jesuit and peace protestor

Daniel Berrigan, to 'know where you stand – AND STAND THERE'. And it will provide you with human, relational, spiritual and political resources as you follow that invitation and take that stand.

The times are urgent, as they have always been. People need God, and as they become dignified and beautiful children of God, people need help. The call of Jesus Christ remains compelling and radical. Ellen and her friends have responded to that call and they're asking the rest of us to do so too. I'm humbled and privileged to be able to work with most of the people who write here, and to follow them on the road of Christian activism.

In short, this is a book for people who want to be resourced as they make a massive difference. I hope you want that too. And trust me – if you read and apply the teaching in this book, your life will become even more interesting. Indeed, you may even get into hot water – but as Ellen would probably say, 'Hey! Come on in! Hot water's fine!'

Paul Bayes
Anglican Bishop of Liverpool

The 12 Rules

1 People before programmes

2 Be useful

3 Collaborate

4 Think BIG – start small

5 Find your level

6 Identify the good things and give the good things away

7 Diversify

8 Make it count

9 Remember where you came from

10 Take risks

11 Travel light

12 Tell stories

Introduction

Being a Christian Activist

... what is good;
and what does the LORD require of you
but to do justice, and to love kindness,
and to walk humbly with your God?
(Micah 6.8)

12 Rules for Christian Activists is an introduction to a way of ordering an active Christian life that makes positive change possible in a world that desperately needs difference-makers.

I have called it a Toolkit for Massive Change[1] because it is my contention that our small, deliberate, purposeful acts of social justice, done in the name of Jesus, will transform God's world. My hope is that having read the stories of everyday Christian activism you will feel equipped to make a difference in your community, and along the way you will:

- pick up tips about how to deepen your social engagement;
- be inspired to be more purposeful and strategic about the work you are doing;
- feel connected to other difference-making Christians;
- be encouraged to tell your story and enable the stories of those around you to be told.

---

1 Mau, Bruce, 2004, *Massive Change*, London: Phaidon Press – I will tell you more about *Massive Change* in the conclusion at the end of the book. This is a great story ...

The inspiration for this book, and the work that emerges from it, came from my thinking and my practice. I am a social activist, and my motivation for this comes from my Christian faith.

The Office for Civil Society defines social action as follows:

> Social action is about people coming together to help im-prove their lives and solve the problems that are important in their communities. It can broadly be defined as practical action in the service of others, which is (i) carried out by individuals or groups of people working together, (ii) not mandated and not for profit, (iii) done for the good of others – individuals, communities and/or society, and (iv) bringing about social change and or value.[2]

Not all social activists are Christians but I think all Christians should be activists. It is on this basis that I wanted to write these Rules.

The Rules are not new, they have been assembled from various places: the grounding of the Old Testament, the life of Jesus and his teachings, the inspiration of the early Church. In addition the rules are influenced by Paulo Freire,[3] Liberation Theology[4] (particularly the writing of Gustavo Gutiérrez),[5] Catholic Social Teaching,[6] the writing of St Ignatius[7] and

---

2 Cabinet Office, 2015, *Social action: Harnessing the potential: A discussion paper*. Retrieved from: https://assets.publishing.service. gov.uk/government/uploads/system/uploads/attachment_data/file/ 411942/Social_Action_-_Harnessing_the_Potential_March_2015. pdf (accessed 15 August 2019).

3 See Rule #6, Identify the Good Things.

4 Ibid.

5 Ibid.

6 See Rule #3, Collaborate; www.catholicsocialteaching.org.uk/.

7 See Rule #11, Travel Light; www.pathwaystogod.org/.

Julian of Norwich,[8] social and community organizing[9] and Asset Based Community Development.[10] You will have your own influences and you will be inspired by writers, activists, politicians and historical figures. But the focus of this book will be the everyday activists who are putting theory into action.

The Rules have also emerged from my practice: as well as being Canon Chancellor at Liverpool Cathedral, I am Director for Social Justice in the Diocese of Liverpool and I have the privilege of hearing and sharing in the social action of many people and communities in the diocese. I am independent chair of the VS6,[11] which is able to represent the Voluntary, Community, Faith and Social Economy (VCFSE) in the Liverpool City Region; I am an advisor for the VCFSE to the Metro Mayor of the Combined Authority of the Liverpool City Region; and a trustee of Micah Liverpool,[12] Together Liverpool[13] and The Liverpool Diocesan Council for Social Aid, which is responsible for running Adelaide House,[14] one of just two independent female-approved premises in England.

What is a Christian activist?

Christian activists are as diverse as the actions we take. Some of us boldly take direct action; some prefer to act gently with

---

8 Ibid.

9 See Rule #1, People before Programmes; www.theology-centre. org.uk/what-is-community-organising/.

10 See Rule #8, Make it Count; www2.cuf.org.uk/research-topics/ abcd.

11 www.vs6.org.uk/.

12 https://micahliverpool.com/.

13 https://togetherliverpool.org.uk.

14 www.adelaidehouse.org/.

a silent strength. We are people from many nations, of different classes, genders and sexuality. Some of us are physically active, others are not. We are extroverts and introverts – all wanting to see social change happen. Some of us get paid to be activists and many of us just want to share our free time. Christian activists are children, young people and old people, some with degrees and others with extraordinary life experience. There are some who feel they are on top of the world and others of us who, frankly, struggle to get through the day.

What we share in common is a heart for social justice. Together we want to see massive change in our communities, our churches and the world. We do these things in the name of Jesus, in the power of the Holy Spirit and by the grace of our creator God. Together we pray for God's kingdom of justice and mercy to be on earth as it is in heaven.

We want to be God's hands and feet in the world and see God's kingdom grow in strength and numbers and deepen in love. We want this world to be a better place for all God's creation. We want to see Christian activism draw people into knowing 'what is the breadth and length and height and depth, and to know the love of Christ that surpasses knowledge, so that you may be filled with all the fullness of God' (Ephesians 3.18–19).

We can do this, and so much more than we can ever imagine, when we understand that 'Alone we can do so little; together we can do so much' (attributed to Helen Keller).

Christian activists don't want to live or act alone, we want to live in communities, seeking the good of all and loving God.

What do Christian activists believe?

The Bible speaks of the boundless generosity of God and the call for the People of God to replicate this. God's vision for the restored kingdom is one of justice and mercy and we are expected to participate in the kingdom plan by ensuring that none are excluded and all are welcomed.

The hard news is that this vision can often seem so far off: our world feels broken and fragile, and humanity appears to be at odds with itself and God. As a result our systems all too often operate unequally, in favour of those who hold power at the expense of the poor, the powerless and the marginalized. The Church has a biblical mandate to change this story and tell of the good news of God's coming kingdom. We need to promote systems that empower, liberate and bring justice to all.

We see in Jesus the person of God who lived a fully human life and engaged in the struggle to bring about his Father's purposes here on earth. As a result, Jesus gave up his life in order to break the old order and bring in the new kingdom. His resurrection and the outpouring of his Spirit enable us to continue his work of generous mercy in the world today.

Christian activists want to take an active role in participating in God's kingdom and they look forward to the time when justice and mercy flow across all the earth. This participation and faith are based in our understanding of the nature of God:

- God is radically generous and we are called to *replicate* this.
- God longs for justice and mercy to be seen in all the earth and for all people and calls on God's people to *enact* this.
- Jesus' ministry *inspires* us to 'learn to do good; seek justice, correct oppression and bring justice' (Isaiah 1.17 ESV).

- Jesus' death and resurrection *confronted* the world order of desolation and isolation from God and *initiated* the coming kingdom of liberation and new life.
- The Holy Spirit *equips* us to join in this new kingdom story, to follow Jesus' example and to live courageous, liberated and just lives to the glory of God.

This way of thinking about God enables Christians to see their lives as inclusive, activist and participatory. We are joining in God's kingdom plan for the earth and including and encouraging others to become part of this story. We are active in our engagement with justice for the earth and all who rely on her creativity to survive. We are willing to participate in the liberation plan and take risks for Christ's sake.

In this sense, all Christians should be activists – though we accept that not all activists will be Christians. This is our calling, but we also know that if we don't (or won't) do this work God will use and transform the good work of people of all faiths and none. This stuff has to be done – and if we don't do it, God will find a way to get it done without us. When we choose to join in God's work of mercy it becomes a collective endeavour – no longer just ours but for everyone – and impacts the whole earth. What makes Christian activism extraordinary is that it is powered by a force beyond human expectation and experience.

I pray that the rest of this book will inspire your activism: in the following chapters you will read the stories of activists who have changed the world for the better and in their own unique ways have made massive change possible. This is the beginning of the collecting together of stories of our Christian activism and social justice. While there is a great deal of diversity here, and various approaches are taken in the collection of stories, there are some missing voices. For instance, though a number of contributors are disabled, we are missing the disability activist voice; there are contributions from black activists in South Africa, but not BAME lay UK activists; and we hear from young social leaders, but the activism of young people and children is not directly referenced. This book is the start of a conversation, the beginnings of the stirrings of a movement. Contributors will share their experience and knowledge with you and offer tips on how to be a Christian activist. These people are my friends and it is a privilege to introduce them to you

First up is Angus Ritchie from the Centre for Community and Theology, who focuses on the rule People before Programmes. This rule reminds us that the systems we operate, the ideas we have and the projects we devise must never be more important than the people who participate, serve or operate them. Our next rule, Be Useful, is a collaboration between two people who have a heart for displaced people: Nadine Daniel and Bonnie Evans-Hills reflect on how our activism needs to be useful not self-serving. Rule #3 is a reflection on the importance of collaboration; like many of these shared stories this rule was negotiated over a cup of tea in conversation with Jenny Sinclair of Together for the Common Good. Rule #4, Think BIG – Start Small, has been written in collaboration with Annie Merry of Faiths4Change. This rule is about how activists must have big ideas for massive change but need to start in a modest way and expect small changes to build into significant action. Rule #5, Find Your Level, focuses on how activists need to work at the most appropriate level in order to be effective. Exploring the principle of subsidiarity in practice, Henry and Jane Corbett reflect on their experience of community activism in a single community over a 30-year period. Rule #6, Identify the Good Things and Give the Good Things Away, explores how we can learn the practice of being generous activists. This rule has been written in collaboration with the Church Land Programme Co-op in South Africa.

Rule #7, Diversify, is a reflection on the significance of diversity and diversification in activism. This chapter is written in collaboration with Kieran Bohan, who is the Open Table network coordinator, and Warren Hartley, who is the LGBTQIA+ Ministry Facilitator at St Bride's Liverpool. Rule #8, Make It Count, explores the importance of evaluating and measuring the impact of our activism. Naomi Maynard of the Church Army and Together Liverpool, Heather Buckingham of the Trussell Trust and I collaborate on this rule and share our working practice and ideas for making our social action count. In Rule #9, Remember Where You Came From, Malcolm Rogers, Canon for Reconciliation in the Diocese of Liverpool, explores the importance of historical perspectives and lived experience for current activism. Rule #10, Take Risks, is a reflection on the need to be courageous and step out with our activism. In this chapter I reflect on my own experience of risk-taking and what it feels like when risk-taking doesn't work out so well. Rule #11 is a reminder that being an activist can be hard work, spiritually exhausting and emotionally draining. Richard Peers, Diocese of Liverpool Director of Education, reflects on the importance of being prayerful, making time to go gently and take time out. Our last rule, #12, is Tell Stories and is, unsurprisingly, all about storytelling. It explores how, as activists, we need to tell our stories and find space for others to tell their own stories. The community theologian Ann Morisy reminds us that at the heart of our activism is the story of Christ.

Each rule is set out as a chapter; the chapter will begin with an outline of the rule and some of the ideas that have inspired it. This will be followed by an exploration of a Bible passage that is indicative of this rule. Most of these Bible reflections have been written by me, unless I explicitly say otherwise. This Bible thinking is designed to stimulate ideas about God and the way we, as the people of God, live and work as Christian activists.

This Bible thinking will be followed by a case study written by one of my activist friends. Each has his or her own style of writing and presentation, so be prepared for changes in pace and proposition. All of these people are experts in their fields and fantastic examples of Christians who live out these rules. I pray their stories will inspire you in your activism and faith. Each chapter will end with tips on how to live out the rule that has been discussed.

The book is designed as a starter toolkit for Christian activism. It should be easy to dip in and out of, and the rules can be read in any order. The purpose of the book is to get ideas flowing and discussion going. You might like to use it as part of a study series or discussion group. You may find that you disagree with some of the ideas shared and want to follow this up with your own thinking and action. If this is the case, then in some ways the book has succeeded in doing what it set out to do – provoke massive change in a small way. This is a book about what happens when we give away our own power and, inspired by the God who loves us, share it as a gift for our community. The heart of being a Christian activist is being part of a diverse, beautiful, glorious kingdom created by our God, who is all in all, and calls us to live by one supreme rule: to love and be loved.

Rule #1

People Before Programmes

Being drawn into community

Angus Ritchie and I met in a café under railway arches in the heart of the parish that he serves in the East End of London. We were meeting to discuss a lecture, 'Populism and the Politics of Jesus', that he was preparing for us at Liverpool Cathedral. His was to be the seventh social justice Micah Lecture hosted by Liverpool Cathedral; previous speakers include Bishop Steven Croft, Bishop David Walker, Bishop Pete Wilcox, Bishop Paul Bayes, Canon Lucy Winkett and Ann Morisy.

Our conversation shifted from the lecture, to family, and on to work commitments, which inevitably led to discussions about our respective writing projects. Angus was just finishing his latest book, *Inclusive Populism*,[1] and I was looking out for collaborators for this book. As we spent time talking about the issues we care about, the people we love and the practices we engage in, it seemed clear to me that Angus would be an ideal person to wrestle practically and theologically with this rule.

---

1 Ritchie, Angus, 2019, *Inclusive Populism: Creating Citizens in the Global Age* (Contending Modernities), London: University of Notre Dame Press.

What we learn from this rule is that God is not shaped in programmes or systems. Our human systems might help us create order and provide security but they do not make lasting change. God is understood, and will be found, in people and in the love shared in community. All the techniques, schemes, organization and so on that we operate for social change mean nothing if they ignore the people who are at the heart of them. People, you-me-us, are what God loves: in the person of Jesus, by the power of the Spirit, we are drawn into community with God.

The rest of this chapter – the Bible thinking, case study and top tips – have been written by Angus.

Boast in the presence of God

Consider your own call, brothers and sisters: not many of you were wise by human standards, not many were powerful, not many were of noble birth. But God chose what is foolish in the world to shame the wise; God chose what is weak in the world to shame the strong; God chose what is low and despised in the world, things that are not, to reduce to nothing things that are, so that no one might boast in the presence of God. He is the source of your life in Christ Jesus, who became for us wisdom from God, and righteousness and sanctification and redemption, in order that, as it is written, 'Let the one who boasts, boast in the Lord.' (1 Corinthians 1.26–31)

St Paul was born in privilege: a Roman citizen (Acts 22.28), a member of the religious and social elite of first-century Israel (Philippians 3.4–6). By contrast, the Church he had been persecuting was led by Jewish disciples who were anything but elite. Most of them had previously been fishermen or tax collectors – following a carpenter from Nazareth who had been crucified as a common criminal. On the road to Damascus, Paul was forced to depend on the very people he had despised and persecuted (Acts 9.1–22). It is here that he learnt that those the world despises are at the very heart of God's saving work – the point he emphasizes to the Christians in Corinth in this passage.

The humility of the early Church reflects the humility of her Lord. Jesus Christ was born in poverty, fled to Egypt as a refugee, and had 'nowhere to lay his head' during his adult ministry. As Paul says, both the cross of Christ and the poverty of his Church are a scandal to the wider world – 'a stumbling-block to Jews and foolishness to Gentiles' (1 Corinthians 1.23).

When he confronted Paul on the road to Damascus, Jesus didn't say 'Why do you persecute my disciples?' but 'Why do you persecute *me*?' (Acts 9.4). If we want to follow Jesus, we must first find him in the faces of the poorest and most overlooked members of his Body.

Well-meaning activism can reinforce worldly hierarchies of power. White, middle-class voices can end up speaking for those in need. Yet in the New Testament, the Church isn't a 'voice for the voiceless' but a place where the previously voiceless speak and prophesy. It doesn't just have 'a heart for the poor'. It has the poor at its heart.

Throughout the Bible and in the history of the Church, the Holy Spirit raises up leaders from, and not just for, those who are oppressed. From Moses and Miriam to Rosa Parks and Desmond Tutu, God chooses the people who experience injustice to bring it to an end. Faithful Christian activism involves joining in this patient work of the Spirit, raising up leaders among the poorest and most marginalized.

As Pope Francis observes, such willingness is in short supply: 'Sometimes I wonder if there are people in today's world who are really concerned about generating processes of people-building, as opposed to obtaining immediate results which yield easy, quick, short-term political gains, but do not enhance human fullness.'[2] This is an aspect of Jesus' practice to which both Church and society continually need to be recalled.

The temptation of impatient activism is to focus only on the programme of issues on which to campaign and not on the people – and in particular, on the 'processes of people-building' that place the poorest at the heart of the process of change.

The most effective antidote to this impatience is prayer – not rushing forward with our own ideas and programmes but stopping to discern where God is already active, and asking for his guidance as to how and where to get involved. As St Paul explains in our reading, it is precisely when we stop boasting in our own power and ability, and instead 'boast in the Lord', that we will have the humility and patience to find out where he is already at work.

Christian engagement in community organizing offers an example of this patient, prayerful work: beginning with the conviction that the poorest are the heart of the Church, identifying the passions and gifts God has given them, and allowing *those* people to develop the programme of action that will develop their confidence and power, and transform their neighbourhoods.

---

2 Pope Francis, 2013, *Evangelii Gaudium: Apostolic Exhortation on the Proclamation of the Gospel in Today's World*, Vatican City, S224.

Community organizing[3]

The roots of community organizing lie in the slums of 1930s Chicago, where Saul Alinsky pioneered this particular form of social action. He was a secular Jewish activist who discovered that churches and synagogues were vital allies in the struggle for justice. He began his work in the 1930s in some of Chicago's poorest neighbourhoods. Jay MacLeod sums up his unique approach:

> Alinsky's breakthrough was to reverse the logic of paternalistic reform by wresting control away from the professional do-gooders and handing it over to the people they were supposed to help. Alinsky transformed community activism from the liberal, elite-led endeavour it had become around 1900 into something he hoped would be more hard-headed and democratic.[4]

'People before programme' was one of Alinsky's key maxims. In this chapter, I will focus on six characteristics of organizing, which offer important insights for all kinds of Christian activism – focusing on developing the power and solidarity of the people who live on the sharp end of injustice.

1 Put relationships before action

At the heart of community organizing is the 'one-to-one' meeting. Both community organizers and the leaders of

---

3 This case study is drawn from a fuller description of Christian engagement in community organizing in Angus Ritchie, 2019, *People of Power: How Community Organising recalls the Church to the Vision of the Gospel*, London: Centre for Theology and Community.

4 MacLeod, J., 1993, *Community Organising: A Practical and Theological Evaluation*, London: Christian Action, p. 4.

churches and other institutions that are in the alliance should be conducting 'one-to-ones' on a regular basis. The purpose of these one-to-ones is to identify and build relationships between grass-roots leaders. Community organizing regards someone as a leader if they have the appetite and ability to do two key things: take action for justice, and identify and develop other leaders.

2 Identify and act on people's passions and interests

The questions at the heart of a one-to-one are:

- What relationships are central to this person's life?
- How do they spend their time and money, and why?
- What are the motivations for key decisions they have made?
- What institutions are they involved in, and why?

Organizing around people's passions and interests is not simply an effective tactic. It is part of taking them seriously: focusing on the realities of their lives and commitments, rather than talking in the language of vague and abstract ideas. In the process of building relationships with our neighbours, and taking action with them for the good of our families and communities, we discover that our hearts are expanded, and our passions and interests becomes less and less self-focused. In losing our lives, we find them.

3 Take local institutions seriously

Institutions attract a lot of suspicion, some of it justified. But an institution is just the set of structured relationships that emerge when human beings agree to be faithful to one another across time. That is what a Scout group, trade union, marriage and mosque have in common. It is one of the characteristic myths of our culture that such commitments restrict our freedom. In fact, our institutions are vital to our freedom. They enable us to build relationships of solidarity and trust across boundaries of age, race and religion. Without them, we are isolated individuals, and our lives and communities are dominated even more by the power of the market and the state. Christians are not called simply as individuals: we are called into the Church, which (as St Paul tells the Corinthians) is not only a visible, earthly institution but the mystical Body of Christ.

Instead of mobilizing people to campaign together on single issues, organizing uses those issues to build a long-term alliance between the religious and civic institutions within a neighbourhood. There is a focus on campaigning on 'winnable issues' so that people unused to any kind of successful action in public life (let alone action with neighbours of other faiths and cultures) begin to have confidence that common action is worthwhile. (The story below of organizing in Manor Park expresses this well.) The alliance develops at the speed they develop. That way, they remain in the driving seat.

In London Citizens, the earliest campaigns were on relatively local issues (for example, the low quality of cleaning and catering at a local hospital in east London), and as the alliance grew through modest campaign successes, it became able to address some of the root causes of the smaller-scale concerns (for example, the impact of the Living Wage Campaign, as it restored a sense of dignity to workers in the National Health Service whose pay and conditions had been cut through outsourcing) and was also able to respond when new challenges and opportunities arose (for example, securing a Living Wage for all involved in the construction of, and work on, the 2012 Olympic Park, and a Community Land Trust on the park as part of the legacy).

4 Don't allow external funders to set your agenda

Community organizing builds local alliances that are financially independent. Their costs, including the pay of salaried professional organizers, are funded as far as possible from annual dues paid by member institutions ('hard money') topped up by grants from charitable foundations ('soft money'). Funding from government – whether federal, state or local – is never accepted. Every year, Citizens UK seeks to increase the proportion of hard money funding its work, so that action is determined by members' priorities: a programme formed by local people and their passions, rather than the targets and agendas of external funders.

5 See action as a way of developing grass-roots leaders

Organizing teaches through experience and action. Problems, once identified, are analysed to identify tangible, winnable demands. Action is not only engaged in to win on the specific issue, but also to develop grass-roots leaders – giving the most excluded and often disillusioned communities the confidence that public engagement can be successful and indeed enjoyable, and building relationships of solidarity and trust across diverse communities. In each new campaign, a community organizer will be considering how the next action could develop capacity in leaders, and evaluation is a key part of their approach to training – teaching the principles of organizing through reflecting on the experiences of success and also the mistakes.

Father Sean's story

Father Sean Connolly's ministry in east London exemplifies this slow, patient process of leadership development: engaging in one-to-one meetings, discerning self-interest, developing the confidence of worshippers who had never previously acted in the public sphere.

Fr Sean arrived in the Catholic Parish of Manor Park just before the London Olympics of 2012 (The parish, in the London Borough of Newham, contained the main Olympic Park.) That year, one of the churches in his parish was celebrating its 150th anniversary. Because of the impending Olympics, the local council was unwilling to put up any new road signage. However, Fr Sean's parishioners felt strongly that their church needed the same public recognition that many other local institutions had already received – and hence that this prohibition was arbitrary and unfair.

These parishioners led a community organizing campaign called 'We Don't Want A Miracle, We Just Want A Sign'. The good-humoured action they took at a meeting of Newham Council got significant local media coverage and led on to an agreement by councillors (the 'target' of the 'action') to provide the sign.

While it was a small victory, it was a very tangible one. Every time parishioners attended the church, they were reminded of what could be achieved by collective action. People who had never before had any experience of successful action to change the behaviour of either government or corporate bodies began to envisage greater possibilities. Five years later, the seemingly trivial victory around a sign has led on to successful campaigns against unjust housing evictions, and in favour of new affordable housing in the area. By beginning with the motivations and concerns of parishioners, and moving only at the pace at which those motivations changed, Fr Sean has managed to achieve far more than if he had rushed into action on a more obviously strategic issue without first developing grass-roots leaders.

6 Don't be afraid of tension

Community organizing recognizes the vital role of tension, teaching that power is never handed over without a struggle. The story of the Living Wage Campaign (see below) has tension at its heart. The purpose of this tension is to secure a new relationship, based on justice and not exploitation.

This use of tension sometimes worries Christians. But it is striking that tension is very central to the practice of Jesus – who, though he loves everyone, is happy to denounce those who abuse their power as 'vipers' and 'foxes', and whose journey from Palm Sunday to Good Friday includes the cleansing of the Temple with a 'whip of cords'. The claim that Christian love is incompatible with tension and conflict does not stand up to any serious examination of the Gospels. In my experience of organizing (for almost 20 years in churches in east London), the practice makes us more and not less faithful followers of Jesus – and challenges our own unwillingness to live with forms of tension and conflict that he seemed happy to use. As one pastor involved in community organizing has put it, 'agitation is a form of love'. We must not be afraid to agitate, so long as the aim of the tension is to build a new relationship founded on justice and mutual respect.

The Living Wage Campaign

Despite sending his office a number of letters from religious and civic leaders, London Citizens had been unable to secure a meeting with Sir John Bond (the Chairman of HSBC) to discuss the poverty wages of those who cleaned the bank's new international headquarters in east London.

The nuns at St Antony's Catholic Church in Forest Gate came up with an idea. The 2000-strong congregation had an account with HSBC. Each Tuesday they deposited a large number of coins in their local branch, because of the many visitors who came into church each week to light candles.

The nuns decided to save up these coins for a few months until they filled a small van. Just before Christmas, with a wider team of London Citizens leaders, they drove to HSBC's Oxford Street branch (in the heart of the capital – and near to BBC Broadcasting House). In full view of the national media, with placards saying 'SIR JOHN BOND – SCROOGE' and 'PAY HSBC CLEANERS A LIVING WAGE', the nuns tied up the branch completely by paying in their coins one by one.

The tension worked: within an hour, Sir John had agreed to meet a team of London Citizens leaders, and in due course HSBC became one of London's first Living Wage employers – and now helps Citizens UK encourage other employers to do the same.

Taken together, these six habits of community organizing have built powerful movements in a growing number of British and American cities. A powerful alliance is being built upon the very citizens who are usually marginalized and ignored. These are the people who politicians often say are 'hard to reach' – whereas, in reality, our political and economic systems keep power out of their reach.

But for Christians, these six characteristics of organizing are motivated by a much more fundamental maxim.

7 Remember, it is God's work before it is ours

Community organizing provides a way in which Christians can place the poorest at the heart of the Church's social action – and can act in solidarity with people of other faiths and none. It is important that our engagement in such social action is rooted in our relationship with Christ. That's why Christians involved in community organizing in east London founded the Centre for Theology and Community. Our mission is to equip churches to transform their communities through community organizing and missional enterprise rooted in theological reflection and prayer.

As Christians, we understand God to be the initiator of all good works – and we believe God to have entered into human history in the person of Jesus Christ. This is what makes Christian engagement in organizing distinctive. Recognized or unrecognized, we believe it is his Spirit who puts justice and compassion on the hearts of those who organize for justice. Therefore our engagement in organizing begins with a 'double listening' – through Scripture and worship we seek to dwell more deeply in Christ, and through listening to our neighbours we seek to discern where his Spirit is at work in the people around us.

In all social action, it is vital to put people before programmes. But that habit is but one expression of a far more fundamental disposition: to recognize that our activism will only bear fruit if it flows from the action of God. 'Unless the LORD builds the house,' as the Psalmist reminds us, 'those who build it labour in vain' (Psalm 127.1). This disposition is expressed in one of my favourite Collects, which is a good prayer for any Christian activist:

Go before us, O Lord, in all our doings
with your most gracious favour,
and further us with your continual help,
that in all our works
begun, continued and ended in you,
we may glorify your holy Name,
and finally, by your mercy obtain everlasting life;
through Jesus Christ our Lord.
Amen.

Tools for the toolkit

- Put relationships before action.
- Identify and act on people's passions and interests.
- Take local institutions seriously.
- Don't allow external funders to set your agenda.
- See action as a way of developing grass-roots leaders.
- Don't be afraid of tension.
- Remember, it is God's work before it is ours.

Books to read

Alinsky, Saul D., 1971, *Rules for Radicals: A Pragmatic Primer for Realistic Radicals*, New York, Vintage Books.

Ballard, Paul; Husselbee, Lesley, 2007, *Community and Ministry: An Introduction to Community Development in a Christian Context*, London: SPCK.

Bond, Becky; Exley, Zack, 2016, *Rules for Revolutionaries: How Big Organizing Can Change Everything*, White River Junction, VT: Chelsea Green.

Han, Hahrie, 2014, *How Organizations Develop Activists: Civic Associations and Leadership in the 21st Century*, Oxford: Oxford University Press.

MacLeod, J., 1993, *Community Organising: A Practical and Theological Evaluation*, London: Christian Action.

Ritchie, Angus, 2019, *Inclusive Populism* (Contending Modernities), London: University of Notre Dame Press.

Ritchie, Angus, 2019, *People of Power: How Community Organising Recalls the Church to the Vision of the Gospel*, London: Centre for Theology and Community.

Solnit, Rebecca, 2016, *Hope in the Dark: Untold Histories, Wild Possibilities*, Edinburgh: Canongate Canons.

Useful websites

Citizens UK, www.citizensuk.org/
Community Organisers, www.corganisers.org.uk/
Centre for Theology and Community, www.theology-centre.org/
Living Wage Foundation, www.livingwage.org.uk/

Rule #2

Be Useful

Handywomen

One of the easiest traps to fall into with activism is that of hubris: thinking we have the answers and believing we are the best people to offer advice or take action is such a great temptation to us activists. This nearly always starts as a perfectly rational and selfless observation around the need to do something about injustice, but so easily we slip into being the expert or the saviour. And therein lies a terrible slippery path of self-delusion that only we can solve the problem and without us the activism will never succeed. This is also why we see different charities or individuals rushing in to try and address injustice without checking where the gaps might be, or who else is working on it and finding ways to collaborate.

This rule was devised as a way to help balance some of these dangers and to create space for discernment and reflection. By starting with looking at our own skills and assets, we can assess what we can offer, and then we set about how we can be most useful and have the greatest impact. Rather than seeing ourselves as the 'great solvers of the problem', we can take a far more modest position and think about how we can be useful.

This chapter features two women who are very useful. Nadine Daniel and Bonnie Evans-Hills are experts in their fields and have great skills. They are part of an ever-growing group who have the concerns of displaced people at the heart of their ministry. The issues that asylum seekers and refugees face in this country and across the world are complex. For many of us, the complexity of the challenges leads to that feeling of not knowing where on earth to start. Nadine and Bonnie have started by being useful, waiting on God to see where their work will take them and trusting that they are playing a useful part in the emerging efforts of many others.

Being ready for every good work

In a large house there are utensils not only of gold and silver but also of wood and clay, some for special use, some for ordinary. All who cleanse themselves of the things I have mentioned will become special utensils, dedicated and useful to the owner of the house, ready for every good work. Shun youthful passions and pursue righteousness, faith, love, and peace, along with those who call on the Lord from a pure heart. (2 Timothy 2.20–22)

This letter is a practical letter. Paul is urging Timothy to do all sorts of useful things – including hurrying to visit him and remembering to bring him his winter coat. He is also reminding him about being spiritually aware and focused – not to listen to false teachers but to be wise like his sister and mother. At the heart of the letter is this call to Timothy to be committed to playing a part in something far bigger than him – bigger than either of their ministries. Using what might feel to some of us like macho imagery, Paul speaks about the power of grace – and the willingness to make sacrifices and endure personal suffering for a greater goal. He likens the spiritual journey to that of a soldier or an athlete or a farmer: it is hard graft, and a labour of faithfulness is full of the hope of Christ.

In the middle of the letter are the verses chosen to illustrate this rule. When I read these verses I can picture the practical utensils in the kitchen, the everyday wooden spoons and stainless-steel knives and chopping boards that we use to get the ordinary things done. Or perhaps the other practical things that make life easier: a vacuum cleaner, feather duster, furniture polish and cloths, the washing machine, fridge and clothes drier. These things seem mundane and ordinary but they really are very useful.

Paul is calling on Timothy to be useful, keep focused, remain motivated, keep his eyes fixed on Jesus and remember his coat. This is very good advice for any activist.

Responding to human need and being useful: two practical stories of activism among displaced people

Our first story is told by Nadine Daniel, who is the Church of England National Refugee Welcome Coordinator. Nadine has a wealth of experience working with displaced people and is an activist who supports many asylum seekers and refugees locally.

'You need my help. How can that work?' In a frantically busy pantry session at Hope+,[1] I could barely hear this offer, let alone process it. It was a hot July day in 2013, and the church we should have been in, St Bride's, a large and cool Georgian church, had been placed out of bounds due to asbestos dis-

---

1 Now incorporated within the charity Micah Liverpool, https://micahliverpool.com/.

covered weeks earlier. Instead, we found ourselves trying to support over a hundred people in St Stephen's, a modern, airless box with room for less than 50. It was chaotic.

Hope+ had opened as a foodbank 'plus' in February. The aim had been to provide a 'holistic approach' to food poverty. By June we were providing food, advice and support for more than 50 local folk, at a time when the national average for a foodbank was 30 people per week. From the start we had tried to recruit volunteers with specialist skills and to partner with useful agencies to attempt to assist people in dealing with the causative factors underlying their food poverty. Food provision was the emergency food aid; the real work lay in disentangling the problems. This took time.

In June 2013, the Home Office cut the per diem stipend for asylum seekers in half. Left to live on £5.28 a day, the asylum seekers housed in assessment hostels within a mile of Liverpool Cathedral heard about Hope+ and came seeking help.

I turned to the speaker, a polite rejection on my lips. Before me stood a Syrian, aged in his mid-twenties and with striking green eyes. To my surprise, he offered his hand.[2] 'I am Nijervan Osman Abdurrahman,[3] and I would like to help. How may I do so please?' My 'Do you speak English?' had to be one of the most crass examples of a statement of the obvious ever heard. Nijervan was too polite to point this out, but instead informed me that he was an English teacher from Aleppo. 'I can speak Arabic too', he smiled.

Nijervan became our first Syrian volunteer at Hope+, and I learnt a valuable lesson. 'Doing to' is patronizing, transactional, and unequal. Hope+ was supposed to be about

---

2 Within Islam, physical contact with members of the opposite sex, such as shaking hands, is uncommon.

3 This was his Arabic name. Once he had his refugee status he took the opportunity to revert to his Kurdish name of Nejrfan.

'being with', helping people to help themselves; and yet at that point, our volunteers were all white, Christian and, to be kind, mostly of a certain vintage. They brought great passion and compassion, and most brought great gifts of listening, patience and resilience. Some brought specialist skills as counsellors and benefit and debt advisers, all much needed in the frantic scramble to offer what support we could to our ever-growing and increasingly diverse guests. That day Nijervan showed me I had to find another way, a way of being with our guests, never losing sight of them in the mess they were in.

On that day, Nijervan came with me as I moved from refugee to refugee, finally able, through him, to gain a better understanding of why they had come to us. And I was appalled. Could Nijervan be translating accurately what he was being told? How could the government treat such vulnerable people so badly? Why were children not allowed to go to school until they were in dispersal accommodation, their allowance cut in half, their housing inadequate, legal aid withdrawn, their families unable to join them? So very many questions for me to find answers to. Where to go, who to ask?

At the end of the two-hour session, we counted the numbers on the vouchers fulfilled that day; 122 people provided with food and some support. Well done us. Not really. I knew it was not enough; it was nowhere near enough. I asked Nijervan if I might buy him a coffee and offered cake as an additional incentive. To my surprise he suggested the Cathedral coffee shop, 'I like it there. It is so peaceful.' The learning had begun.

Over coffee, Nijervan spoke of his desperate need to do something, anything. He felt helpless and frustrated. In that first of many conversations with him, I learnt all the major failings of our no-longer-fit-for-purpose asylum and immigration system. Then he asked a question: 'Can you help me and others like me to help those who need more help?' What he wanted was for me to show him the system and how to negotiate it – basic things like how to open a bank account, where to find free wi-fi, how to flourish rather than simply survive.

The following week I asked the existing volunteers if they would help train some of the refugees and asylum seekers to work alongside them. Over 90 per cent agreed, the others left. That was painful, but it was necessary. Another lesson learnt: people volunteer for many reasons, not always the most helpful ones. Then we went looking for help. Networks, I had already learnt, were important. Many local schemes fail for the lack of a support network. Displaced people have such a complexity of issues, it is simply not possible to know how to help with all that besets them. Far more important is knowing where and who to ask. I spoke to everyone, from the City Council to Christian Aid and the British Red Cross. With the latter we started a clothing and household goods bank to run alongside the foodbank, and advice provision. We recruited legal advisers from the university and local law firms.

After a few months, Nijervan was 'dispersed', in the bland jargon of the Home Office, to Manchester. This, I learnt, was a deliberate policy to prevent the asylum applicants from becoming settled: they should be made to feel as unwelcome as possible. Feeling helpless, we said our goodbyes. Three weeks later he was back. He had saved 50 pence from his daily allowance so that he could come every three weeks to help. At other times we would phone him to interpret (he also spoke Kurdish Kurmanji), or e-mail a document for translation. Through him we found other Syrians to help with translation. Never did I expect to spend so much time discussing the Metaphysical poets or Restoration drama with young Syrian men. Their thirst for knowledge was insatiable, as was mine. What a treat.

For those of the volunteers with a faith, whatever that might be, most would acknowledge that it had been enriched and strengthened by working alongside those of other faiths. Inevitably, curious questions are asked of one another: Why do you worship three Gods when there is one? What is this *Jinn*, the Holy Spirit? Why do you become Jihadis? Why do you wear a hijab?

More recently the government committed to the Vulnerable Persons/Children Resettlement Scheme, and with it, Community Sponsorship, to enable refugees to be housed in previously monocultural areas. Local Councils struggled to offer support and turned to faith-based organizations for help. Suddenly there was an opportunity for areas of the country without refugees to welcome them. But how to do that without the infrastructure readily available in places such as Liverpool or Cardiff?

When the post of National Refugee Welcome Coordinator was advertised, I felt that all I had learnt at Hope+ could be used on a national scale. In preparing for my interview, I was surprised to discover the number of rural parishes and communities heavily involved in refugee resettlement. I was blessed by being offered the job, and I set off to meet these communities. How had they made it work? There was in truth a fair degree of do-goodery, of wanting to do what was right. There is nothing wrong with this at all. What is important is how that calling to do what is right and good is translated into walking alongside, of being with.

The joy of these resettlement schemes is that they bring communities together. They are doubly transformational. There is also a role for anyone who wants to get involved. As one redoubtable Scouse lady, well to the north of 70, said to a Council Official wrapped in jargon, 'It's not rocket science, love, anyone can make a home, and offer a welcome to someone who needs it.' They also demonstrate to the wider community that the folk in the pews are also the folk rolling their sleeves up and doing something – something that people who think they have no interest in what happens in church might want to become involved with, just as they do with foodbanks, community food markets, asylum support. In doing that, they see what the church folk do, and they also learn why we do it. Suddenly this practical demonstration of faith has the power to transform those lives too. But do it together, or as Archbishop Worlock and Bishop Sheppard said, 'We do things better together.'

With our help, Nijervan had his Syrian degrees validated and accredited. He was offered a sponsored post-graduate MSc in Linguistics at the University of York and has just submitted his PhD thesis on Semitic languages (April 2019). Having lost his entire family, he has married a fellow Syrian Kurd who had also lost hers. They are happy and settled.

Being with can be hard, it can be frightening, but it is what we are called to do. Above all, 'Do not neglect to show hospitality to strangers, for by doing that some have entertained angels without knowing it' (Hebrews 13.2).

Our second story is told by Bonnie Evans-Hills, who is an Anglican priest, and acts as coordinator for the UK Coalition, working with the UN Office for Genocide Prevention.

This thoughtful reflection from Nadine Daniel highlights a number of issues for those seeking to work with refugees. But more importantly, Nadine has presented a human face, with all the complexities life brings, and more. Each and every individual refugee has a unique story that needs to be told, needs to be heard and needs to be healed.

When we receive and provide assistance to those seeking refuge, whether here in the UK, in the EU or elsewhere, it is a work of reconciliation for a life that has been lost.

When someone shares their personal story, they make themselves vulnerable – will anyone will be patient enough to hear their story through, will they be heard with sympathy and respect, will they be believed, and can any help be offered in the way of immediate humanitarian aid, in helping to settle and begin life anew, and in finding justice? There is a process of mourning for the loss of what has gone before – a home, a sense of safety, a family, a livelihood, possibly a life before torture, before rape and before witnessing the horrific death of those around them. The privilege of listening to these stories is a gift to us.

And listening is our responsibility. Can we listen with earnest and honest sympathy? During the 2014 Global Summit on Ending Sexual Violence in Conflict, held in London, I listened as a support worker for women who have been raped told me of the abusive process these women are forced to endure as they go through their asylum claims. We know how difficult it is for anyone who has been raped to tell their story. There is an incredibly painful element of shame involved. Their story must be believed if any kind of investigation is to be carried out. But we also know that every time they tell their story they are reliving that assault, reliving the shame, reliving the pain. So when questioning takes place it must be done sensitively. But when it comes to asylum claims, the default position is one of scepticism: the claimant must prove every single detail. They are continually asked to repeat their story – in order to be certain they have not changed any details. Hence the two things essential to healing when it comes to rape or torture of any kind – believing the testimony of the survivor, and not asking them to continually live through the pain by repeatedly being asked to tell their story over and over again – are absent from the process.

When we are working with those seeking to claim asylum or who already have refugee status, listening also means not asking people to relive a painful period of their life until they are willing and ready to share it. When speaking to Holocaust survivors and their children, I often hear that some never share their stories, wanting to live their lives in the here and now, the present, rather than remember past suffering. For others, it has taken decades before they felt ready to share with their children and family what they had been through – let alone with anyone else.

There is a man, Hasan Hasanovic, who works at the genocide museum at Potticelli, outside Srebrenica in Bosnia. He is a child survivor of the genocide and spends his life carefully telling his story. It takes a lot out of him every time he tells it. He once told me of a time he was giving a talk in the USA to a group of university students and a young girl started crying quite loudly. He said it made him angry, and he asked her afterwards why she was crying so hard. He wanted to understand whether she had also been through a tragedy of some description. But she said she was just very moved by his story. It upset him. He felt that he had the right to shed tears, but not her – that the pain was his, and she could not have understood what he went through. However sympathetic we might feel about someone's story, we must remember the story is theirs to tell, and not ours. They are not sharing their pain for our entertainment. They are sharing it so that someone knows, so that we can do something about it – help them, and ensure this kind of thing never happens again. But of course, genocide and atrocities do repeat themselves, over and over again. What we can do is to help and support the human being before us.

And this is where it comes to justice, to reconciliation of lives. Healing is not something that happens and then is done. Healing is a process. We cannot take away what has happened. And we cannot take away, not individually anyway, the threat that means people cannot return to the homes they knew. Those will always be gone. What we can do is to help pick up the pieces. But as in any work of reconciliation, the priority is the needs of the survivor. As Nadine outlines so clearly, it is not about doing something for others but rather about enabling them to do for themselves and walking alongside them.

Sometimes it is about removing stumbling blocks along the way. With regard to our asylum system, and the continuing hostile environment, one of the things we can do is to advocate for a just, fair and equal system that provides genuine support to those in distress and those who have undergone trauma. Sometimes it is about speaking out against discrimination and the populist hate speech that is so prolific in our current climate. And sometimes it is about just sitting down with someone and getting to know them over a cup of something warm and comforting.

There have been recent stories of Home Office officials not believing that some of those seeking asylum are Christian, and increasingly clergy and church leaders are being asked to attest to someone's faith. Oftentimes the immigration official has little to no understanding themselves of what constitutes Christian faith.

Revd Ray Gaston, whose congregation consists of many who have migrated or sought asylum in the UK from a number of backgrounds, has provided a gently sensible guide to working through validity of conversion claims – advice which he states has received grateful response from asylum judges. He uses what he states is a process devised by Bishop Lesslie

Newbigin, former bishop of the Diocese of Madurai-Ramnad in India. He asks three questions: 1) Does this individual have a personal relationship with Christ? 2) Do they participate in a worshipping community or church? 3) Do they have a story of faith? What brought them to faith, whether an immediate conversion, as in the way of St Paul, or that of the greater majority of people, a Road to Emmaus conversion – a process of possibly years on a journey of faith?

Each and every individual I have met who has made a claim to asylum based on faith has an answer for each of these – each of them has met Jesus along the road of life in some capacity; each of them has sought out others, companions on the way; and each of them has a unique story of their journey. I am not so naive as to believe there will not be those who somehow make something up that is less than genuine. Some may have started out that way, but that level of deceit is difficult to carry out on a day-to-day level and with the pressure so many are under. Those who are less than genuine tend to drift away before long. By removing any demand they may perceive to convert, by respecting the belief they already hold to and enabling them to live that belief out to the best of their ability, we also remove any feeling some may have of a need to deceive in order to survive. The help is offered, whatever their belief, because they are an individual in need.

The passage from the Second Letter of Timothy speaks of the best household utensils being the ones that are 'cleansed' of impurity and dedicated to good work. Within this is an implication that it is the good works of the tools and not their material that makes them special to their owner. I am reminded of one couple I interviewed not long ago. He had converted to Christianity in a house church in Iran and his wife was furious with him for it, as it put their lives and their marriage in danger. Eventually he was found out and had to flee the country, and she with him. They walked from the south of Iran to Dunkirk, where they camped out over a winter, before being accepted for asylum in the UK, first in Birmingham, and then in the city where I met them. The fear on their faces was still palpable, and they were keen not to be identifiable. Throughout their journey, each kept their respective faith, but when they reached Birmingham the wife decided to attend a church, and then asked to be baptized. This is not a story about being triumphal, this is a story of the kind of faith, whatever faith it is, that leads you out of danger, to walk thousands of miles in destitution and hunger; the dedication it takes for a married couple to remain faithful to one another in such circumstances. This is faith. And this is the kind of faith that will feed us here, we who struggle to get up on a Sunday morning.

Tools for the toolkit

Nadine's tools

- Be Prepared – to be taken by surprise by something you were not prepared for. We are all wonderfully and fearfully made in God's image; that makes us complex.
- Be Honest – to acknowledge that you don't always know all the answers, but by trusting in God you will find an answer even if it isn't the one you thought you wanted.
- Be Generous – to your fellow toilers in the vineyard, without whom little can be achieved in serving God in the image of those displaced and most in need.

- Be Welcoming – to all who come seeking your help, but who will leave you with far more of God's grace and wisdom than you could ever give them.

Bonnie's tools

- Listen – hear the voice of God in the sounds of God's creation.
- Walk alongside – discover the footprints of Jesus made in the sand by the feet of your companions.
- Serve – serve them, wash their feet.
- Love – in that loving you might just discover God's love for you in return.

Books to read

Betts, Alexander; Collier, Paul, 2018, *Refuge: Transforming a Broken Refugee System*, London: Allen Lane.

Bonhoeffer, Dietrich, 2015, *The Cost of Discipleship*, new edition, London: SCM Press.

Brown, Malcolm; Chaplin, Jonathan; Hughes, John; Rowlands, Anna; Suggate, Alan, 2014, *Anglican Social Theology: Renewing the Vision Today*, London: Church House Publishing.

Charlesworth, Martin; Williams, Natalie, 2014, *The Myth of the Undeserving Poor: A Christian Response to Poverty in Britain Today*, Surrey: Grosvenor House Publishing.

Gustine, Adam L., 2019, *Becoming a Just Church: Cultivating Communities of God's Shalom*, Downers Grove, IL: IVP.

Houston, Fleur, 2015, *You Shall Love the Stranger as Yourself: Biblical Challenges in the Contemporary World*, London: Routledge.

Scott, Ruth, 2014, *The Power of Imperfection: Living Creatively With Human Complexity*, London: SPCK.

Snyder, Susanna; Ralston, Joshua; Brazal, Agnes M., 2015, *Church in an Age of Global Migration: Pathways for Ecumenical and Interreligious Dialogue*, London: Palgrave Macmillan.

Spencer, Nick, 2016, *Doing Good: A Future for Christianity in the 21st Century*, London: Theos.

Tutu, Desmond and Mpho, 2014, *The Book of Forgiving*, London: Collins.

Wells, Samuel, 2015, *A Nazareth Manifesto*, Chichester: Wiley.

Wells, Samuel; Coakley, Sarah, 2008, *Praying for England: Priestly Presence in Contemporary Culture*, London: Continuum.

Wells, Samuel; Rook, Russell; Barclay, David, 2017, *For Good: The Church and the Future of Welfare*, Norwich: Canterbury Press.

Yoder, John Howard, 1972, *The Politics of Jesus*, 2nd edn 1994, Grand Rapids, MI: Eerdmans.

Rule #3

Collaborate

A mighty collective

The old adage goes that 'There's no I in TEAM', but this can easily negate the reality that teams are made up of individuals who have chosen to share the challenge of collaborating together. Being in collaboration with others is a decision an individual makes in order to seek a common end. When we collaborate we become a team and the competition becomes a shared experience. We get to share the glory and the risk, and when things don't go well we also share the lack of success.

Working with our skills in collaboration with others is what makes being the people of God exciting. Being part of the body of Christ is what makes us inseparable and strong. Together we are a mighty collective; apart we are lonely strangers in a strange land.

This chapter is about how we work together for the common good. We will explore the work of Jenny Sinclair and Together for the Common Good, and seek to discover how collaboration can rehumanize and reconnect dislocated individuals and restore communities.

A miraculous collaboration

On the third day there was a wedding in Cana of Galilee, and the mother of Jesus was there. Jesus and his disciples had also been invited to the wedding. When the wine gave out, the mother of Jesus said to him, 'They have no wine.' And Jesus said to her, 'Woman, what concern is that to you and to me? My hour has not yet come.' His mother said to the servants, 'Do whatever he tells you.' Now standing there were six stone water-jars for the Jewish rites of purification, each holding twenty or thirty gallons. Jesus said to them, 'Fill the jars with water.' And they filled them up to the brim. He said to them, 'Now draw some out, and take it to the chief steward.' So they took it. When the steward tasted the water that had become wine, and did not know where it came from (though the servants who had drawn the water knew), the steward called the bridegroom and said to him, 'Everyone serves the good wine first, and then the inferior wine after the guests have become drunk. But you have kept the good wine until now.' Jesus did this, the first of his signs, in Cana of Galilee, and revealed his glory; and his disciples believed in him. (John 2.1–11)

The first miracle of Jesus takes place at a wedding in Cana. This is a story of fruitful collaborations: not just between the newlywed couple but also between Jesus and his mother, Jesus' mother and the servants, the servants and the chief steward, and the steward and the bridegroom. The miracle of this miracle is the relational, blessed collaboration of all participants! Without each person playing their part, the story fragments and the party ends. But the story is really about justice – specifically about justice as the outcome of effective collaboration.

A wedding was, as it is today, a significant event in the lives of the couple, but this extended beyond the individuals themselves and was also very important to the whole community. Everyone was caught up in the event. So it was hardly surprising that Jesus' mother was invited – and that Jesus and his friends would also be part of the celebrations.

Very quickly the story turns to the problem: the wine has run out and the only person who seems to notice that there is a problem is Mary. Mary notices the wine has run out – and she is worried because wine running out isn't just an inconvenient thing that means that the party might have to stop. It's far more significant than that. The wine running out would mean terrible shame for the family of the wedding couple and for the couple themselves. It would make them socially unacceptable; they would be humiliated and Mary knows this.

So Mary turns to Jesus because she knows he can do something about the injustice. She knows that if anyone can help avoid the shame of social stigma, Jesus can. But Jesus didn't think he was ready to take on injustice, ready to offer 'signs' to the people about who he was; he felt he wasn't ready for his 'glory' to be revealed.

But notice what Mary does. Mary ignores him. Mary doesn't argue with him, she doesn't debate the matter with him. She just becomes part of the solution – she makes the injustice stop. She takes part (she collaborates) in the miracle and tells the servants to do whatever Jesus asks them to do. Then she backs off and lets Jesus take over.

Jesus asks the servants to fill six stone water-jars – big massive jars – all filled to the brim with water. Those jars weren't ordinary jars, they were part of a ritual of purification used to make sure that each guest was purified as they went to the feast. They were not just clean in terms of being rid of germs but completely clean inside and out and so free from sin and pure before God. This purification was an important part of Jewish preparation before eating. So those jars were very special indeed. And they are also a sign – a sign that 'God is doing a new thing within the old Jewish system, bringing purification to Israel and the world in a whole new way.'[1]

The servants did exactly what he asked them to do – and somewhere between their putting the water in the jars and the pouring out for the master of the feast, a remarkable thing happened. Jesus deals with the injustice; he changes the shame into glory and water into wine. Indeed, he doesn't stop there, because this is no ordinary wine. This is beautiful wine – the best wine. Jesus didn't come just to make things all right – he didn't live, die and be resurrected so that people could just have OK wine at parties. No, Jesus came so that we might have life in all its fullness (John 10.10).

What does the master of the feast say to the bridegroom? 'Everyone else serves the best wine first, and after the guests have drunk a lot, he serves the ordinary wine. But you have kept the best wine until now!'

Jesus not only restores the bridegroom's social standing but he extends his reputation. Jesus' own glory is reflected in the glory that he gives to this unnamed bridegroom. This whole story of the first miracle of Jesus is wonderful, grace-filled collaboration.

---

1 Wright, Tom, 2002, *John for Everyone*, Part 1, London: SPCK, p. 22.

Together for the Common Good (T4CG) – in conversation with Jenny Sinclair

The Together for the Common Good prayer

This prayer is available to download from the T4CG website. T4CG suggest that each person in the group read a line each and that the first and last lines are said altogether.

Glory be to the Father, the Son and the Holy Spirit +

Come Holy Spirit. We welcome you here in our midst.
Govern our hearts and minds, govern every aspect of our time together.
Be in every thought and word; in every intention and motive.
Lord, we thank you for those who have been an inspiration to us.
Thank you for calling us through the Gospel to work together, and for each other.
We pray for others working for the Common Good and for those who resist it.
Bind us together across our traditions and move our heart's desire closer to the heart of your desire for us.
Lord, give us the grace to do your will, and make our mission a joy.

In the love of Jesus Christ our Lord, Amen.

I met Jenny Sinclair in 2015 at Alsop High School in Walton. At the time I was the parish priest of a small church in the area and I was working with local activists on a community social engagement project. We sat round a table in the staff room, along with Peter Bull the Head of Religious Studies, community worker Dave Coates and Jenny's colleague, the Liverpool scholar and social justice activist Professor Hilary Russell. Peter had convened this unlikely group of people to collaborate on a small grass-roots project that aimed to build the capacity of young people through the theme of 'Hope'. We were meeting because Peter and I had become interested in Jenny and Hilary's work on Common Good thinking as a way to explore some of the difficult issues that the young people of the area were facing. This meeting was the first of many and it marked the beginning of a complex and exciting collaboration.

Jenny is the founder of Together for the Common Good.[2] The charity is marked by its ability to live out its principles and work at the most appropriate level according to the need of the task. Dedicated to strengthening the bonds of social trust, T4CG is part of a wider movement reimagining culture to overcome division and put people, communities and relationships first. Its work involves promoting Common Good thinking with and for different groups and individuals, calling people to fulfil their vocational responsibility by putting Common Good principles into practice.

T4CG is volunteer-driven and partners with people across the churches, producing teaching materials for schools, training materials for lay people and church leaders, Bible studies and other resources.[3] They also bring Common Good thinking into public and civic life through talks and public conversations as well as by networking across church, social and political arenas to influence and offer Common Good narratives and perspectives on current affairs.

---

2 https://togetherforthecommongood.co.uk/.
3 https://togetherforthecommongood.co.uk/.

Common Good thinking

Principles to put into practice:

1 The Common Good
2 The Human Person
  – Human Dignity, Dignity of Work, Respect for Life, Human Equality
3 Social Relationships
  – Solidarity, Subsidiarity, Participation, Reconciliation
4 Stewardship
5 Everyone is included, no one is left behind[4]

I knew when I talked to Jenny about Christian activism, and particularly her thinking about Rule #3, that she would bring her Common Good thinking into our conversation and offer a rich multi-layered perspective. Most of this conversation about collaboration and Christian activism took place over a very long lunch at the Wash House Café in central London (which is itself a space for community members and others concerned with social justice and activism – the 'best kept secret for lunch in Westminster').[5]

Jenny is the daughter of Bishop David Sheppard, the sixth Bishop of Liverpool (1975–97), and the writer and broadcaster Grace Sheppard. Jenny spent her teenage years in Liverpool and was later influenced by her father's commitment to urban ministry and his 22-year public partnership with the Catholic Archbishop of Liverpool, Derek Worlock. Curiosity about

---

4 T4CG has designed this framework to make the basic principles of Catholic Social Teaching more widely accessible. For details see T4CG website: http://togetherforthecommongood.co.uk/.

5 https://cafe.theabbeycentre.org.uk/

their ecumenical collaboration turned out to be a call of the Spirit that unexpectedly brought Jenny into public life. This, together with her own conversion to Catholicism (in 1988), has given her the courage to pursue what she describes to me (misquoting Fr Austin Smith) as becoming a collaborator with God, in his 'great creative participation'. She explains that finding her vocation in T4CG in collaboration with others has given her 'focus and purpose' and has 'made sense of years of un-focus'.

At the heart of any exciting collaboration is the unpredictable fruit of the relationships formed. Certainly the partnership between Sheppard and Worlock could not have been planned or the outcomes predicted. They arrived in Liverpool just six months apart and immediately understood the imperative before them. There was a vacuum of credible civic leadership at a time when unjust structures were blighting people's lives and weakening communities. The city was scarred with a history of sectarianism, degraded infrastructure, high unemployment and low business confidence.

In Sheppard and Worlock the city gained two people who together forged a national reputation as advocates for social justice. Standing side by side, their body language demonstrated they were acting for the city, rather than in the interests of their own institutions. Despite their seriously held doctrinal differences (Sheppard was an Evangelical Anglican and Worlock a Catholic), they saw themselves as brothers in Christ and dedicated themselves to strengthening communities and local institutions. The ecumenical collaboration of these two 'good and faithful servants' birthed a new model of church leadership for the Common Good: a carefully calibrated non-partisan position[6] characterized by bridging

---

6 See Filby, Eliza, 2015, *God and Mrs Thatcher: The Battle for Britain's Soul*, London: Biteback.

divides and working with unlikely allies. Their collaborative approach healed divisions, opened doors, cultivated local leadership and attracted investment, creating a national platform for engagement in the public square where issues of inequality and social justice could be addressed.

Jenny does not like the term 'activist' and does not think of herself as one. Her concern is that the term limits the field – the perception that 'activism' is a minority political activity, whether left or right, deters the majority from getting involved. Rather than the preserve of a dedicated fringe, Jenny believes the call to civic engagement needs to be mainstream for all the people of God. While the vast majority of Christians want to make a constructive contribution, the potential of the Church to effect social transformation remains still largely untapped. She believes the call to be 'missionary disciples'[7] is a call to every single person to fulfil his or her unique God-given vocational responsibility.

Nevertheless, despite her dislike for the label 'activist', Jenny agreed to collaborate on a chapter in a book about activism – and this is at the heart of what collaboration is about; that is, not necessarily working with those you agree with on all points but together exploring ideas that may throw up extraordinary possibilities and run the risk of challenging the expectations of those who take part.

It is my contention that collaboration – and the finding of personal purpose within collaboration – is integral to the common life of the people of God. As Christians, our lives are marked out by our willingness to collaborate with each other and with God. Finding our unique discipleship niche – what

---

7 Pope Paul VI, 1975, *Evangelii Nuntiandi: On Evangelization in the Modern World*, London: The Incorporated Catholic Truth Society; Pope Francis, 2013, *Evangelii Gaudium: The Joy of the Gospel*, London: The Incorporated Catholic Truth Society.

God is calling each of us to be – is what makes us step out of our individual concerns and creates capacity for building the Common Good with others.

Christian activism is about being conscious actors in the story of God's purpose to bring justice and mercy to the world. The people of God are called to be different; we are called to be far more than nice and good. We are called to be justice makers and mercy givers – particularly in relationship with those who are rejected, excluded, those we do not know or who do not share our affiliations. The Common Good is not a utopian ideal; it is about the shared life of a society – what happens between us – and sometimes 'what happens' is messy, complex, beyond our control and may not be easy.

As I type these words, the UK parliament has voted again to reject a deal for Brexit. Whatever the pros and cons, the debates that are ongoing not just in the House of Commons but in the front rooms of our houses, in pubs and in other private and public spaces of the nation would be transformed if they were infused with Common Good thinking and Common Good practice. Building the Common Good is not about finding middle ground, nor is it about coercing people into a forced consensus driven by one group dominating. It is about the transformation that happens through participation, negotiation, mutual respect and working out ways to flourish together.

The Common Good is the shared life of a society in which everyone can flourish – as we act together in different ways that all contribute towards that goal, enabled by social conditions that mean every single person can participate. We create these conditions and pursue that goal by working together across our differences, each of us taking responsibility according to our calling and ability.[8]

Key to Common Good thinking is the acknowledgement that we are made in the image of our relational God – Father, Son and Holy Spirit – and as such we are designed to thrive in relationships. Common Good thinking helps individuals and communities focus on our shared humanness and overcome the forces intent on driving us apart. It is an approach that rejects the dehumanizing tendencies of both totalitarianism and extreme individualism and, correctly understood, critiques political ideologies of both the left and the right. Jenny argues that Christians need urgently to overcome tribalism and resist falling into the liberal versus conservative values divide[9] now exposed and threatening to destabilize the Western world.

In a time of social division, broken trust and political upheaval, it may well be that Christian activism for the Common Good can be a part of the solution. But Jenny laments that too many Christians can be found lining up on one side or the other, even joining in the acts of mutual contempt. This raises serious questions of credibility and poses a

---

8 See T4CG's definition of the Common Good at www.together forthecommongood.co.uk.

9 See Goodhart, David, 2017, *The Road to Somewhere: The Populist Revolt and the Future of Politics*, London: C. Hurst & Co.

challenge to the mission of the Church: how can we hope to be a force for unity if we ourselves are divided? In an article in *The Tablet*, Jenny refers to Paul's letter to the Ephesians, in which he calls for the unity and reconciliation of the whole of creation through the agency of the Church.[10] Are Christian activists willing to cross the line and practise a radical inclusiveness – to be open to collaboration with those affiliated to a different political persuasion, class, background or doctrine?

In fact, collaboration across our differences is not only desirable but necessary for our civilization to thrive. The American psychologist Jonathan Haidt has found that liberal and conservative views reflect different personality types and tend to make different points of moral emphasis, explaining why they talk past each other. If we are to rebuild a sense of social solidarity and strengthen the bonds of social trust, he argues, we must not retreat into echo chambers. Indeed, to get to a shared sense of the truth and to solve problems in a sustainable way, both left and right perspectives are required and should be intentionally pursued. Collaboration is necessary.[11] Haidt goes further and warns that a society endangers itself by insulating opposing views from each other. The 'safe space' phenomenon and 'deplatforming' in this sense are therefore the enemy of collaboration, and of the Common Good.

For Jenny, when St Paul says we should tell each other the truth, for we are members one of another (Ephesians 4.25), he is telling us that without each other's free contribution our life together is incomplete. If Christian activism is to play its

---

10 Sinclair, Jenny, 2017, 'Rebuilding the Broken Body', *The Tablet*, 6 April, www.thetablet.co.uk/features/2/9729/rebuilding-the-broken-body.

11 Haidt, Jonathan, 2013, *The Righteous Mind: Why Good People Are Divided by Politics and Religion*, London: Penguin.

part in building the Common Good, it must be characterized by a commitment to a shared life, and by a hospitality where people know they will be heard and are able to speak freely. In an era in which some communities feel ignored and held in contempt, the Church ought to be a place that is characterized by belonging and respect, offering a sense of family for everybody. No one should be discarded; everyone is needed.

Jenny believes that this involves reasserting what it means to be a human person, to unveil the sacred nature of our shared community. Our intentional collaboration across our differences can act as a powerful antidote to the degradation of human beings into group identities or products to be bought and sold in the marketplace. Indeed, the esteem in which the Christian tradition holds the human person means it is well placed to fuel a counter-cultural insurgency.

At the core of the action of collaboration is the desire to participate in the relational heart of God. We are loved by God completely, simply because of who we are as human beings – not because of what we produce, nor for our beliefs, backgrounds or distinguishing characteristics. Similarly, the significant relationship God seeks is the one between us and God – this is what centres us as individuals. Our identity is found in this relationship with God, and it will liberate us, create agency, connect us deeply with each other and creation, and will bring us infinite opportunities. Prayerfully opening up ourselves to collaboration in God's great creative participation will generate in us a desire for deep collaborative activism with others.

Tools for the toolkit

- Don't rush to action. Prayer comes first – listen to the Spirit. Be patient – that sense of urgency you feel is not from God.
- Meet with a spiritual director several times a year. Get plenty of sleep. Beware the 'violence of activism' (Thomas Merton).
- Relationships always come first, and always before action.
- Have a one-to-one conversation every day with someone you don't know. Listen more than you speak.
- Thorough preparation pays off. Use lists as much as you find helpful. Make a new list every night for the following day. It will help you sleep.
- Involve the people you seek to help from the beginning and do not take over. Beware the perils of middle-class church.
- Keep your centre of gravity in the Christian tradition, refuse to be tribal and resist political ideologies.
- Do not attempt to do everything on your own. Ask for help but keep your expectations reasonable.
- Look for unlikely allies – you could pray, 'Lord, show me who you want me to work with.'
- Encourage people around you to fulfil their vocational responsibility, while also fulfilling your own as best you can. Celebrate other people's successes.
- Intentionally build bridges between people who are estranged in order to strengthen social trust.

- Intentionally build bridging capital between local institutions (invite people to a shared meal and hear their perspective). This strengthens civil society.
- Aim for everything you do to have a rehumanizing influence – resist the dominance of capital and of the centralized state, both of which have a tendency to dehumanize.
- Test if your initiatives are Common Good by running them under the lens of the Principles. Build your capacity with Common Good training. Find out more on the T4CG website.

Books to read

Bartley, Jonathan, 2006, *Faith and Politics after Christendom: The Church as a Movement for Anarchy*, Milton Keynes: Paternoster Press.

British and Foreign Bible Society, 2017, *Calling People of Goodwill: The Bible and the Common Good*, Swindon: Bible Society Resources.

Dwyer, Judith (ed.), *The New Dictionary of Catholic Social Thought*, Collegeville, MN: Liturgical Press.

Filby, Eliza, 2015, *God and Mrs Thatcher: The Battle for Britain's Soul*, London: Biteback.

Goodhart, David, 2017, *The Road to Somewhere: The Populist Revolt and the Future of Politics*, London: C. Hurst & Co.

Haidt, Jonathan 2013, *The Righteous Mind: Why Good People Are Divided by Politics and Religion*, London: Penguin.

Pope Francis, 2013, *Evangelii Gaudium: The Joy of the Gospel*, London: The Incorporated Catholic Truth Society.

——, 2018, *Gaudete et Exsultate: On the Call to Holiness in Today's World*, London: The Incorporated Catholic Truth Society.

Russell, Hilary, 2015, *A Faithful Presence: Working Together for the Common Good*, London: SCM Press.

Sagovsky, Nicholas; McGrail, Peter, 2015, *Together for the Common Good: Towards a National Conversation*, London: SCM Press.

Sheppard, David, 1975, *Built as a City: God and the Urban World Today*, 2nd edn, London: Hodder & Stoughton.

——, 1983, *Bias to the Poor*, London: Hodder & Stoughton.

——, 1984, *The Other Britain*, Northampton: Belmont Press.

Sheppard, David; Worlock, Derek, 1988, *Better Together*, London: Hodder & Stoughton.

Smith, Austin, 1983, *Passion for the Inner City*, London: Sheed & Ward.

——, 1990, *Journeying with God: Paradigms of Power and Powerlessness*, London: Sheed & Ward.

——, 2010, *Mersey Vespers: Reflections of a Priest and Poet*, Stowmarket: Kevin Mayhew.

Winstanley, Gerrard; Benn, Tony, 2011, *A Common Treasury*, London: Verso Books.

Useful websites

Catholic Social Teaching, www.catholicsocialteaching.org.uk/.

Pathways to God (Jesuits in Britain), www.pathwaystogod.org/.

Together for the Common Good, http://togetherforthecommon good.co.uk.

Rule #4

Think BIG – Start Small

Eating an elephant

I remember when I was 15 and just about to start my GCSE revision – I was completely overwhelmed and panicking. It was the kind of panic that led to inertia and fear. I couldn't even begin to study so I did nothing – for quite a long time. Eventually I confided in a teacher, and I must have looked like a frightened creature because she very gently asked me what I thought was a stupid, unhelpful question: 'Ellen, what's the best way to eat an elephant?' My frightened-creature face transformed into the face of a bewildered teenager as I replied sarcastically: 'I have no idea? Why on earth are you asking me that?' She said calmly: 'The only way to eat an elephant is … one mouthful at a time! Now, write a list of what you need to do and work through it slowly until you finish.'

Thankfully, I did as she advised. I used the time that was left to slowly, step by step, do enough revision to pass my exams and just about get away with it.

There are some problems, issues or challenges that seem completely overwhelming, and as activists we have no idea where to start, let alone how on earth we will make any significant change. Things like global warming, financial inequality, food poverty, health and well-being instability and gender inequality can seem so immense, systemic and beyond our capacity to challenge that we just give up before we even start. But the advice of my GCSE teacher is just the same for us activists who want to be part of massive change. Don't be put off by the enormity of the change you want to see in the world. Make a plan and eat that (metaphorical) elephant one bite at a time. This chapter is about how you go about making massive change happen. We will look at how a few activists have gone about thinking big and starting small. They will offer tips on how to plan, act diligently and make each step patient and sure.

I have written a reflection on a short Bible passage with a big vision, and the rest of the chapter tells of the work of Faiths4Change.[1] It has been written by Annie Merry, who is the CEO of the organization, and she reflects on their ambition to encourage us to live more responsible, just and creation-connected lives. The focus is on how the organization enables churches to explore what it means to actively embed the fifth mark of mission into all areas of church life, both within and beyond the parish, including in partnership with others.

Faiths4Change have a big vision but they know that individuals, churches and communities can easily become overwhelmed by the enormity and complexity of the ecological and equitable task ahead of us. So they work slowly and steadily with others to nurture and encourage relationship building and sharing, undertake collective and equitable actions, learning and celebrations that support and deliver small, sustainable but significant changes that strengthen our interdependence with all of creation and deepen our commitment to live lightly.

---

1 www.faiths4change.org.uk/.

Go into all the world

And [Jesus] said to them, 'Go into all the world and proclaim the good news to the whole creation.' (Mark 16.15)

The last verses in Mark appear to be a bit out of joint with the rest of the Gospel. Most commentators think that some later editors of the Gospel felt the first ending was too abrupt and not what really happened. The argument goes that the disciples couldn't possibly have 'said nothing to anyone' about Jesus' resurrection because otherwise how could the good news have got out! So two additional endings were added to make the point that Jesus' story was told and people came to believe in the hope of redemption after the resurrection.

These two alternative endings are usually set in brackets at the end of the Gospel. In the first bracket is a short pithy end that marks out the next step of the Church as it proclaims salvation to the east and west. The second bracket is a bit longer and stylistically more like Matthew and Luke's Gospel endings. In this we are told that the women grasp the good news of resurrection first, they share this with the other disciples, and then the resurrected Christ speaks to them all in person about what their next mission was to be. It is in this teaching, in the third ending of the Gospel, that we hear of the BIG mission plan: 'Go into all the world and proclaim the good news to the whole creation.'

That's it – that's the big mission plan. Eleven men and an unknown number of women were being sent out into all the world to let all of creation know about redemption through Jesus. There was no mention of a map or a schedule, no financial planning was put in place and nobody appeared to be put in charge. The mission was impossible! How could this small group of people possibly manage this BIG vision? But they were promised validation by signs and miracles, so they just got on with it – one encounter at a time. And because of the tenacity of that small group of disciples and friends, Jesus' story got out and good news was heard, lives changed and they keep being transformed even today.

We are a part of creation, not apart from it

Never doubt that a small group of thoughtful, committed citizens can change the world. Indeed it's the only thing that ever has. (Attributed to Margaret Mead)

My name is Annie Merry. I am the CEO of Faiths4Change. We have a big vision to nurture, learn, share, develop and grow a deeply committed and actively engaged interfaith network to mitigate the impact of climate change and increase the resilience of our communities, with partners from all sectors, as we face climate emergency. From the strategic level to the individual, we can all live justly with the fifth mark of mission embedded in all we do: *to strive to safeguard the integrity of creation, and sustain and renew the life of the earth.* We know that this is a big ask, so we encourage people to take small purposeful steps towards this ecological commitment and change the world one shared action at a time, from food growing and sharing to reusing resources, learning and inspiring each other. This is the story of Faiths4Change, which I pray will inspire you to think big and start small.

The Five Marks of Mission

The mission of the Church is the mission of Christ:

1 To proclaim the Good News of the Kingdom
2 To teach, baptise and nurture new believers
3 To respond to human need by loving service
4 To transform unjust structures of society, to challenge violence of every kind and pursue peace and reconciliation
5 To strive to safeguard the integrity of creation, and sustain and renew the life of the earth

The Five Marks of Mission are an important statement on mission. They express the Anglican Communion's common commitment to, and understanding of, God's holistic and integral mission. The mission of the Church is the mission of Christ.[2]

Faiths4Change began initially as a three-year, multi-faith, environmental pilot project called Operation EDEN in the Diocese of Liverpool in 2004–7. The thinking behind EDEN was BIG – it was founded on the common ground of caring for the environment shared by people of all world faith communities and people of goodwill, on research that demonstrated that faith communities were strongest in areas of greatest need, and through dialogue led by the former Bishop of Liverpool, the Right Reverend James Jones, in consultation with senior representatives of different Christian denominations and different world faiths – Islam, Judaism and Hinduism – on Merseyside.

2 www.anglicancommunion.org/mission/marks-of-mission.aspx.

Bishop James wanted to grow a network of environmental representatives from every Anglican church who would lead small-scale environmental partnership projects with local residents, people from other Christian denominations, other world faiths and different sectors. By being small scale, partnership projects addressed specific needs in different communities. For example, one church, Christchurch, Anfield, and its neighbours, volunteered to tidy, dig, mow and plant the gardens of local elderly residents; they also painted railings and undertook several litter picks. By working together they developed neighbourly relationships, shared skills, transformed their local environment and at the heart of their actions is their love of God and creation.

Many small actions made up each of the 56 projects supported during EDEN, leading to a patchwork of community environmental transformations across the Diocese, and to a big difference.

EDEN supported the 56 projects with a total of £110,000 in grants to faith community partnered projects; the projects attracted £160,000 in match funding, 1,514 volunteers and 100+ partners.

Norris Green Fingers – inspired by the vision of three parishioners and the vicar at St Christopher's Church, Norris Green – was the first EDEN-supported project in 2004. Norris Green Fingers brought together elderly gardeners and local people of all ages to share, learn and grow together by transforming a 0.1 acre patch of church land into a thriving community allotment.

The success of EDEN led to further funding support from the RDA, continued support from the Diocese of Liverpool, and support from faith communities to develop and establish a roll-out across the North-West to Burnley (Mosque); Preston (RC College) and Manchester (St John's Church, Trafford), and led to a new name – Faiths4Change. Between 2007 and 2010, Faiths4Change supported a further 70 projects and engaged with a more diverse range of faith communities and local people. Projects included working with Preston Forum of Faiths to create a statement on different faith perspectives on the environment and climate change; research with a Muslim scholar on Quran recycling options; installing cycle racks at a Manchester church; and an environmental art exhibition.

Small actions can lead to a bigger difference. Start a ripple: sit quietly and pray, allow yourself to be led or take simple small actions in church/at home:

- Walk to church and invite others to walk with you.
- Along with a cup of tea and a chat after service, have a donations table/area that people can contribute to; encourage reuse.
- Make refreshments fair trade.
- If you're offering lunch, make it a local, organic, animal-friendly meal.[3]
- Make cyclists welcome at services/lunch/coffee mornings by, for example, identifying an area for bikes to be locked up, buying a puncture repair kit and providing simple tools.
- Provide free tap-water refills and get on the map by signing your church/church building up to Refill.org.[4]
- Stop buying single-use plastics. Consider buying refillable water bottles and reusable cutlery, utensils, plates and mugs. If you have to use disposable items, source compostable alternatives.
- Encourage/support/lead your church to sign up to Eco Church, A Rocha UK's award scheme for churches in

---

3 www.christian-ecology.org.uk/loaf/.
4 https://refill.org.uk/.

England and Wales who want to demonstrate that the gospel is good news for God's earth.[5]

- Join Green Christian, a network organization formed in 1981 in order to share green insights with Christians.[6]
- Share what you are doing with many others and learn from them too.
- Find out about and join other groups and networks, such as Faiths4Change Faith and Climate Network (incorporating Eco Diocese).
- Celebrate.

In 2010, significant changes in the funding and geopolitical landscapes resulted in a decision to establish Faiths4Change as a registered charity and registered company limited by guarantee, to close the Preston and Manchester bases and maintain the Liverpool and Burnley ones. It also focused the purpose of the charity and set it on a new path.

Faiths4Change charitable objects

1 To promote for the benefit of the public the conservation, protection and improvement of the physical and natural environment, and in particular to bring together faith communities to work towards improving the environment of disadvantaged communities within the North West of England.

2 To advance the education of the public in the conservation, protection and improvement of the physical and natural environment, particularly within disadvantaged communities in the North West of England.

---

5 https://ecochurch.arocha.org.uk.
6 https://greenchristian.org.uk/.

Faiths4Change is still rooted in the values of its founders, in the common beliefs and practices of all world faith communities in caring for the earth and all of its communities; Faiths4Change believes that this is strongly interdependent with social justice. People who live on low incomes are more likely to live in areas where there are higher levels of air pollution and limited or no access to green space; to experience food insecurity, limited access to fresh, affordable food and have higher incidences of long-term ill-health, to name a few barriers. These are all barriers to creating an inclusive, responsible, just and environmentally sound society.

The environment offers a much-needed social platform for people to come together in a gentle way to overcome barriers by growing community and connection; to improve physical, social, mental and spiritual health together by undertaking identified and needed practical environmental projects, such as weaving a network of art sessions with different groups using unwanted resources, which culminate in a community-wide exhibition; creating a community garden in which to grow fresh food to cook and share regular meals together; and larger-scale work, such as flood-risk awareness in diverse urban communities.

Our work is supported through successful grant applications; service-level agreements with larger organizations; the development and delivery of not-for-profit chargeable services that mainly focus on connecting people and land; an amazing team of staff, volunteers and trustees. We are a Living Wage Foundation Employer.

In 2014–15, an independent evaluation of our work identified that we worked with 9,895 beneficiaries, the majority of whom could be considered marginalized or vulnerable.

Between 2010 and 2019, we worked with thousands of people across Merseyside and Greater Manchester, mostly with faith partners, to create and deliver almost 130 projects that act as social platforms to bring people together to care for the earth and each other. Projects encompass all strands of living responsibly, from raising awareness about flood risk to cooking and sharing food together; from pop-up donated clothing boutiques with repair stations to growing food for community lunches – it's always a partnership approach.

Since 2014, we've been active members of Cool Wirral, Wirral's climate change strategy group. A key strand of the climate change strategy is focused on faith community-led action. With council and faith community engagement in 2017, we began to explore the need for a network to share issues and actions around climate change and begin to develop themed climate action events for Interfaith Week and beyond. The Faith and Climate Network is a fledgling project that aims to enable people of different faiths and denominations to share teachings, ideas, campaigns and practical actions with each other.

Our lead on Eco Diocese with the Diocese of Liverpool has emerged from the wider faith and climate actions and through the commitment of Bishop Paul to the 'Go for Gold' Eco Diocese award at the beginning of 2019. Our approach is a team one, engaging clergy, lay members and related organizational leads such as the Merseyside Christian Aid Coordinator and the Merseyside Environmental Trust Deputy Chair. In January 2019, the Diocese had one bronze awarded church – St Martin's, Southdene, Kirkby – and no registered churches. Just six months later, we have 37 registered churches, five awarded churches and at least three churches actively working on their bronze and silver awards.

The different strands of faith and climate activity have also enabled us to develop deeper partnerships for action. At Liverpool City Region level, we are members of the

Year of Environment Steering Group and joint lead on the climate change listening event that will inform the city region environmental strategy. At grass-roots level we're engaged in joint working on climate action with Friends of the Earth, Transition Town, Zero Carbon Liverpool and others.

Bringing statutory, grass-roots and faith connections together is offering much learning and a wider reach, as well as a more joined-up partnership approach on climate actions across Merseyside and a clear message to all we meet: all world faiths offer guidance for people to live in harmony with each other and the planet through belief in God; although how this is understood varies, the essence is the same – the earth and its communities are one and sacred.

At neighbourhood level we're currently working in Bolton, Bury, Rochdale, Kirkby, Skelmersdale and Liverpool. One of our longer-term projects is with St Michael's in the City, Upper Pitt Street, Liverpool.

The church has a small, elderly congregation and is on a small housing estate in an area with very little green space, close to the city centre. Through relationship building and a gentle opening of the door with a community lunch and reuse arts activities offer, we've just completed a design together for approximately 40 per cent of the church land (which had been overgrown and overtaken by bamboo for many years).

The community garden offers a shared a vision of the church land being used for the wider community, including a prayer and reflective space, a den area and food growing. The land is being utilized to offer a practical welcome to local people, to breathe new life into the church, share teachings on caring for creation in practical gentle ways and grow the church's role in serving the community. We're now offering two full days of activities each week with and for the local and wider community – Mondays and Thursdays. Thursdays are in-the-garden days, with a morning session focused on connecting with and enhancing urban nature, and a partnership with Myerscough College in the afternoon offering funded City and Guilds Horticulture qualifications for adults on a drop-in weekly basis.

Challenges

I think that the biggest challenges I face are ones that relate to trust in God's plan and doubt: trust in God that all is working as it should; even though in my heart I know it to be true, I still sometimes suffer doubt. As an organization, it's similar: even concerns about income, projects and partnerships also stem from the same root – trust. And I think trust relates to truth, which in turn is God.

I would describe myself as a faith-rooted activist principally connecting to Christianity, and other world faiths and belief systems, through teachings and practices that relate to a deep connection with creation. For me, the essential root and starting point is to see everything as a part of a whole, whether this is people, plants, oceans and earth, or injustice, insecurity, unfair trade and poverty. The whole, in its completeness, is infinite, beyond our full understanding and created by God. This is the big vision that drives me as an activist.

I have been exploring Christian mindfulness, yoga, meditation and reading around Christian beliefs for a number of years. I've been particularly inspired in recent times by reading the Mennonite Doris Janzen Longacre's book *Living More With Less*.[7] Although written many years ago, it is possibly even more pertinent today, as we understand the

---

7 Longacre, Doris Janzen, 2010, *Living More With Less* (30th Anniversary edition), Harrisonburg, VA: Herald Press.

negative impact that human beings have had on creation, from reduction in insect populations to people dying as a result of extreme weather conditions.

Through daily practice I'm gaining more clarity of purpose in life, having a sense of being held, loved and supported but also challenged to push beyond a comfortable space to seek the truth and act positively, particularly in relation to climate emergency. In essence this means living as simply as possible, considering the impact of my actions and continuing to explore how the tools of community, stories, silence, prayer, nature, rituals enable my deepening connection with God.

Climate action is one of the most pressing challenges that we face. Activists across the world are coming together in order to speak out and encourage systemic change. The task in front of us seems almost insurmountable and so vast that it can paralyse us and leave us unable to know where to start with our action. This reflection has offered some gentle ways of taking small steps, setting achievable goals and acting carefully in solidarity with others.

Tools for the toolkit

- Pray/meditate/be quiet regularly: focus your prayers and hold the stillness as a time to give thanks and ask for discernment as to ways you can take further action.
- Understand your own biases: we are not always able to be rational because of the biases we hold. Being able to understand these biases helps us to make better decisions and act with more care.

- Listen to the views of those whose actions/policies you oppose – you need to understand all of the arguments in order to inform your argument and actions.
- Speak the truth: in a world where truth is not always clear, equip yourself with as many facts as possible and speak with honesty and clarity.
- Research and connect with others: fill the gaps in your understanding with the experience and knowledge of other people. Collaborate (see Rule #3) with as many people as possible – even those you don't agree with!
- Be peaceful even in disobedience (women arrested for actions at Greenham Common sang peace songs in court).
- Be bold: you can do this; we can do this together!
- Act now: if you feel strongly about something, act with courage and act now. Don't wait.

Books to read

Berry, Thomas, 1991, *Befriending the Earth: A Theology of Reconciliation Between Humans and the Earth*, Mystic, CT: Twenty-Third Publications.

Bookless, Dave, 2010, *God Doesn't do Waste: Redeeming the Whole of Life*, London: IVP.

Bradford, Louise, 2019, *Save the World: There is No Planet B: Things You Can Do Right Now to Save Our Planet*, London: Summersdale Publishers.

Clawson, Julie, 2009, *Everyday Justice: The Global Impact of Our Daily Choices*, London: IVP.

Foster, Claire; Shreeve, David, 2007, *How Many Lightbulbs Does it Take to Change a Christian? A Pocket Guide to*

Shrinking Your Ecological Footprint, London: Church House Publishing.

Jones, James, 2003, *Jesus and the Earth*, London: SPCK.

King, David; Walker, Gabrielle, 2009, *The Hot Topic: How to Tackle Global Warming and Still Keep the Lights On*, London: Bloomsbury.

Porrit, Jonathan, 2013, *The World We Made: Alex McKay's Story from 2050*, London: Phaidon.

Stanley, Bruce, 2013, *Forest Church: A Field Guide to Nature Connection for Groups and Individuals*, Powys: Mystic Church Press.

Stuart, Tristram, 2009, *Waste: Uncovering the Global Food Scandal*, London: Penguin .

Summers, Rachel, 2017, *Wild Lent*, Stowmarket: Kevin Mayhew.

——, 2018, *Wild Advent*, Stowmarket: Kevin Mayhew.

——, 2019, *Wild Worship*, Stowmarket: Kevin Mayhew.

Valerio, Ruth, 2008, *L Is For Lifestyle: Christian Living That Doesn't Cost the Earth*, London: IVP.

Useful websites

A Rocha, https://arocha.org.uk.
Faiths4Change, www.faiths4change.org.uk.
Forest Church, www.mysticchrist.co.uk/forest_church.

Rule #5

Find Your Level

Subsidiarity and solidarity

One of the key struggles of any activist is to determine where we will be most effective in making change for good. Discernment around where to focus action and the most appropriate level on which to operate is vital to the way activists work. Do we work locally for change or do we lobby at the highest level? Who do we ask for assistance and from whom do we seek solidarity? For me the principle of subsidiarity is what guides my discernment and helps me to make decisions about who to consult, how to collaborate, where to seek assistance and how to allocate resources.

> The principle of Subsidiarity states that the individual and the family precede the state; that is, individuals do not exist for the state but rather the state exists for the well-being of individuals and families entrusted to its care. Furthermore, nothing should be done by a higher or larger organization that cannot be done by a lower or smaller one.[1]

In this chapter, Henry and Jane Corbett reflect on their struggles to work at the most appropriate level and how they have

1 Dwyer, Judith (ed.), *The New Dictionary of Catholic Social Thought*, Collegeville, MN: Liturgical Press, pp. 927–29.

campaigned locally, regionally and nationally for the rights of people in their community. They explain something of the challenges of local campaigns and the significance of standing in solidarity with those who want to effect change. Even if this is not your personal struggle, it may be that within your community it is a presenting problem that you find yourself faced with, or that this is a social justice issue that you feel strongly about. You may not need to collect a food parcel from the foodbank but you may choose to stand in solidarity with those who do. Finding ways to provoke local change for good is usually about discovering the local resolution to the presenting need; it rarely needs a grand intervention or national strategy.

I worked with Henry as his curate in the parishes of St Peter's and St John Chrysostom, West Everton, for a number of years, and the three of us continue to share stories of social justice and often act together in solidarity with local campaigns. This chapter was discussed and planned over cups of tea at Henry and Jane's kitchen table – a safe space to discuss anything and plan massive change. Henry and Jane have written the rest of this chapter, the Bible reflection and top tips, and have shared their story of being community activists in West Everton in Liverpool.

'What is it you want?'

The words of Nehemiah son of Hakaliah: In the month of Kislev in the twentieth year, while I was in the citadel of Susa, Hanani, one of my brothers, came from Judah with some other men, and I questioned them about the Jewish remnant that had survived the exile, and also about Jerusalem.

They said to me, 'Those who survived the exile and are back in the province are in great trouble and disgrace. The wall of Jerusalem is broken down, and its gates have been burned with fire.'

When I heard these things, I sat down and wept. For some days I mourned and fasted and prayed before the God of heaven. Then I said:

'LORD, the God of heaven, the great and awesome God, who keeps his covenant of love with those who love him and keep his commandments, let your ear be attentive and your eyes open to hear the prayer your servant is praying before you day and night for your servants, the people of Israel.' (Nehemiah 1.1–6 NIV)

People become activists for all sorts of different reasons. Grief is one such reason: a much-loved child is run over on a quiet residential road by a car going at 30 mph, and the family in their grief become activists to get a 20 mph limit on that road so that no one else should suffer and grieve as they have had to do. In Everton, our local primary school was under threat of closure and a parents' action group was formed to save a school for our community; then the group helped set up a wider group to save other schools in a schools' reorganization in the north end of Liverpool.

For Nehemiah it was the sadness of hearing that 'the wall of Jerusalem is broken down, and its gates have been burned' (Nehemiah 1.3). He sits down and weeps. He mourns and fasts. It's not right that Jerusalem is in that state. The walls should be standing strong and the gates should be in position: this is Jerusalem, rightly judged for the wickedness of past days with its people scattered into exile, but now many of the exiles have returned and the city should be restored.

And his grief turns to action, as it did for the child's family and the parents of our primary school under threat of closure. Nehemiah's first action is prayer: is he on the right track when he thinks this situation is sad and shouldn't happen? Yes, he recalls God's promise that 'if you return to me and obey my commands, then even if your exiled people are at the farthest horizon, I will gather them from there and bring them to the place I have chosen as a dwelling for my Name' (Nehemiah 1.9 NIV).

Then his second action is a carefully thought-out plan. He wants to get back to Jerusalem to repair those walls and those gates. He is the cup-bearer to King Artaxerxes. Who can give him permission to leave that job in Susa and who can give him a letter to help his safe conduct and another letter to get him some timber to help the restoration work? In any campaign that is a key question: who takes the decisions, who can give the permission for the campaign to succeed? In Nehemiah's case the level he needed to work at was that of the king himself, Artaxerxes, and as cup-bearer he had unique access to the king. A relevant question in any campaign: who is the best person or group to approach as key decision-maker or permission-giver?

So Nehemiah approaches the king, and does so with a sad face – a dangerous thing in the king's presence. It begs the question 'Why sad?' and Nehemiah graciously says, 'May the king live for ever!' and then explains: 'the city where my ancestors are buried lies in ruins, and its gates have been destroyed by fire' (Nehemiah 2.3 NIV). The reference to his ancestors is a shrewd nudge that this is not just a personal issue but something bigger than just Nehemiah: respect for ancestors was a powerful concern in Artaxerxes' culture.

The king then asks the golden question, 'What is it you want?' In any campaign, clarity about what the individual or group wants is important. And Nehemiah is very clear. He prays and then answers with the requests above: permission to go, the letters and resources he needs, and a time limit for his return, with a gracious 'If it pleases the king' (v. 4).

So Nehemiah's campaign is under way. He gets to Jerusalem, quietly by night he inspects the walls and the gates, and he gathers supporters. This time he works at the level of any who will join the action: the high priest Eliashib, priests, nobles, different family groups, different district rulers, goldsmiths, merchants.

There is opposition and ridicule: how often do activists hear the words 'You've got no chance!' Nehemiah calls meetings to keep accurate communication and good practice going, he prays for strength, he resists some intimidation tactics and he is wise in refusing those 'scheming to harm me' (Nehemiah 6.2 NIV). In many a campaign there is often a group who don't want the change and will try and weaken, accuse and intimidate the activists: 'they are only doing this for their own glory' or maybe a brick through a window, or an anonymous note through the door. Nehemiah and his supporters kept going and 'So the wall was completed ... in fifty-two days ... with the help of our God' (Nehemiah 6.15–16 NIV).

'Nothing about us, without us, is for us'

The book of Nehemiah was the subject of our preaching at St Peter's in Everton during a local campaign in the 1980s. Liverpool City Council had proposed for our West Everton area a large Everton Park, a big lake and the demolition of 17 tower blocks, an estate and also 30 good four-bedroom houses. But what did local people in West Everton think? In the 1950s and 1960s, local people had been moved to outlying estates and new towns without any consultation when the tower blocks and the Arkwright Street estate had been built in place of the old terraced streets. Local people then, along with the vicar, had pointed out the problems of high-rise living for families. Now, in the 1980s, would local people again not be listened to?

The appropriate level at which to start was a questionnaire around the area to ask the opinion of the people in the community what they thought of these plans. So West Everton Community Council (WECC) set up the questionnaire and a group of local activists, including Jane and me, other church members from St Peter's and from the local Catholic churches, and also people with no church affiliation, went door-to-door to record people's views. With over 500 responses, the overwhelming majority said that there should be an Everton Park at the top of Everton hill as the tower blocks blocking the view for 30 years were coming down, but that the community down the hill should be kept together, with better housing on offer rather than a big lake, thus protecting local schools, shops, facilities and that precious thing, community spirit. All agreed that the 30 good-quality four-bedroom houses on and around Langrove Street should be kept.

To consult, listen to and involve those most affected by any plan is surely the most appropriate starting point. So the view of the residents was obtained. But often there is a wider picture: would the demolition of the houses and a larger park with a big lake serve a greater good? The City Planning Officer was a person of known integrity and widely respected. What was his view of the clear results from the WECC questionnaire? His wisdom was quietly sought and his considered view was that the local residents' majority opinion of a park at the top, the 30 houses saved, other housing added on and no big lake made excellent sense.

The campaign somewhat miraculously succeeded. Members

of the Langrove Street Action Group squatted in one of the four-bed houses to prevent demolition; we requested and received encouraging support from the city's church leaders, both Anglican and Catholic; a court order to stop demolition temporarily was obtained through a local solicitor; and the City Council were taken to court over lack of consultation. The court case was then lost, as technically the Council had 'consulted the community' (but not acted on their views!), but 47 Councillors were disqualified from office for not setting a Council rate and the new Council was willing to agree to saving the houses and to adopt in large measure the plan of the local community. From the local level to the City's Planning Officer to a local solicitor to a disqualification from a high court! From the cup-bearer to King Artaxerxes; in God's eyes every person is made in God's image and so to be valued and respected.

Other important campaigns in our Everton area have been for a new local health centre, for further improvements to our local housing, for a community-led family support project, which became the first Sure Start centre in Liverpool, for a good local supermarket with healthy food available, for local employment, for the ongoing improvement of Everton Park, for appropriate support, including a foodbank for people in poverty alongside anti-poverty campaigns, as well as for the saving of the local primary school mentioned above. In each case it was vital to work first at the level of those most affected and then at the level of the decision-makers and to resist those who might try and twist a campaign for their own ends. Two other campaigns further illustrate the importance of working at the most appropriate level: the Radcliffe Action group and the campaign to protect asylum seekers from bullying.

The Radcliffe Action group was formed following grief and anger over a suicide and a rape on the Radcliffe estate.

The estate had been built in the late 1970s and won an award for its design, modelled on a Cornish village. However, the design, with its criss-crossing walkways and its ingenious mix of housing, was a gift to the money-making drug-dealers of the 1980s heroin trade. You could enter the estate from the south side and be quickly lost as you attempted to come out on the north side. If you could afford a car, a rare event in Everton in the 1970s and 1980s, then you couldn't park it outside your front door: it would have to be parked on the outside of the estate before you walked in to your home via the maze of pedestrian walkways. The local joke was that a social worker who went searching for a family in January would still be looking in July. Sadly, no local residents were involved in the design of the soon infamous Radcliffe estate. A Sunday tabloid ran a centre page spread on 'Smack City', with pictures of the estate and stories of young children as runners for the profiteering drug-dealers.

Then came the rape and the suicide: a small group of us got together and West Everton Community Council leafleted the estate with notice of a meeting, open to all residents, on the edge of the estate in a community hut. The police thought no one would come because of threats by the dealers. Our group thought if ten come, that is a group to work with. Over 100 residents came and then the local wisdom kicked in: don't start any campaign against the drug dealers and users and runners, as that will only inflame the situation and could possibly set one family member against another. There was a presenting problem that was causing the estate to become a centre for the heroin trade: the Cornish village layout. So working at the most appropriate level with the Radcliffe estate residents, West Everton Community Council, with Radcliffe residents very much involved as members of that body, campaigned for the estate to be redesigned. The City Council were lobbied, persuaded, and a Housing Association came on board and the infamous Radcliffe estate was replaced with excellent housing in clear streets, which you could look up and down, where no social workers got lost, and there were no more centre-page spreads of children being used to run drugs from ice-cream vans. The local Catholic priest did a study of how local families were deeply affected by a member becoming addicted to heroin, and the Radcliffe Action group, through local wisdom, had not been responsible for putting one family member against another. The heroin problem did not disappear from Everton, but no longer was the Radcliffe estate a magnet for drug dealing and drug use.

In the 2000s, two emptied-out tower blocks near St Peter's suddenly became occupied by asylum seekers. The blocks had been bought for next to nothing by a businesswoman, and after a few months of trying without much success to fill the block with residents, she somehow got a contract to take on asylum seekers from Kent. Without preparation, and with a background of inaccurate media coverage about asylum seekers in some national newspapers, our Everton area had people from Iraq, Zimbabwe, Sierra Leone and Afghanistan living in the community, some with little English, many with serious trauma in their recent experience, and living in two tower blocks where conditions were poor and overcrowded and where the owner, not local herself, was totally unsympathetic to their needs and aggressive and bullying in her approach.

Myself and a local Christian friend, Matt, had visited the two blocks delivering our community newspaper the *Everton Telegraph* (aka the 'Everton Telly'). I have edited this newspaper for many years as part of my work with St Peter's church and the Shrewsbury House Youth and Community Centre (aka the 'Shewsy') where I am warden. It was Christmas time and so the headline had been 'Jesus was an asylum seeker', with his flight from the angry, threatened Herod. Through that friendly contact with the Everton Telly, Matt and I had got to know a good number of the asylum seekers, including a young man, Arkan, from Iraq, whose Muslim father had told him before being killed by Saddam Hussein, 'Christians can be good people.' So Arkan rang me with the request: 'Henry, can I do your church a favour? We want to use the church as a sanctuary while we go on hunger strike about the way we are being treated.'

I had no clue how to respond beyond saying, 'Right, Arkan, let's talk about that: do call round to the vicarage. I'll put the kettle on', and then ringing my wife Jane, at that stage very much involved with local activism and with WECC in particular (and later a local Councillor for our Everton ward). Jane quickly rang our local Member of Parliament, Louise Ellman, and also the local Police Race Relations Liaison Officer.

So in our back kitchen were Arkan with nine other Iraqi men, our MP, the police officer, Jane and myself. We listened, and in the Shewsy community centre there were two dormitories with accommodation for 12 people. A phone call to a Shewsy Board of Management member gave the thumbs up for the dormitories to be used to accommodate the ten men so that they didn't have to return to an angry, bullying landlady, and the campaign to improve their situation began. The first level was to hear their concerns, their stories and their hopes. That was achieved round the vicarage kitchen table and in the days to follow in the Shewsy and in the church. The *Everton Telegraph*, going to every home in the parish, told the true story of an asylum seeker's situation as they sought safety in our community. Arkan told his story to the young people in the youth club, and much of the initial animosity ('Who are these people?!') was dissipated.

The next appropriate level was for Louise Ellman to receive the petitions Jane had worked on with other local churches and to raise in Parliament the issue of mistreatment by the landlady/owner. It was a great moment when Arkan and his friends watched on television Louise stand up on the government benches and mention their nightmare block and call for the contract to be taken away. The campaign succeeded, the blocks were emptied out, and subsequently they were bought and refurbished by a property developer who listened respectfully and didn't allow any block buying of the flats for profit by disinterested parties.

Sadly, at another level the campaign was not so successful: Arkan, his friends and many of the other asylum seekers would have liked to stay in Liverpool, but representatives from the National Asylum Support Service (NASS), again seated around our vicarage kitchen table, were strangely resistant to listening to Arkan's appeals. Arkan's English was fluent, but the NASS official would turn to me and say 'Can you tell Arkan that they need to move to Sunderland ...' No arguments would change their mind, and MP Louise could disqualify a bullying landlady with a block in an unfit condition but couldn't get NASS to be more sympathetic and flexible in where they placed suffering asylum seekers. Every long-term activist knows the experience of not winning every campaign.

The principles of our community work in West Everton are to:

- work alongside, rather than on behalf of
- serve rather than control
- share vision rather than impose it

- be there for the long haul rather than the short stay
- build strong relationships that look outwards rather than cliques that look inwards
- manage conflict while transforming it into positive action
- share power rather than take it
- form partnerships built on trust, mutual respect and understanding
- treat people on the level and
- have 'tough minds and tender hearts'.

(Jane Corbett)

Henry and Jane's experience of working locally and engaging in regional and national campaigns demonstrates the importance of finding the appropriate level for our activism. There will be times when the most significant work will need to be done locally – indeed, the principle of subsidiarity is important here, remember: 'nothing should be done by a higher or larger organization that cannot be done by a lower or smaller one'. However, remaining local and utilizing the influence of higher or larger organizations to effect change may also be necessary. Collaboration, networking, reaching out in solidarity to other communities and campaigners can make all the difference. As activists, we must think about where we have the greatest leverage and influence – and find the most appropriate level of power and influence to make change happen. Always keeping focused on the local issues that concern real people will enable national campaigns to sustain credibility and focus.

Tools for the toolkit

- WECC's motto: 'Nothing about us, without us, is for us.' So it is fundamental to consult, listen to, involve those most affected by the issue that you are grieving over, angry over, concerned to campaign over. 'Who does it affect? Consult them, involve them.'
- Prayer in activism is partly about attending to God's perspective, where there are no 'The great and the good' but each person is equally important and if someone is being bullied, then God is on the side of the bullied against the bully. If someone is unfairly not being heard, then God is on the side of their voice being heard. It is not about 'giving people a voice'. They have a voice: it is a matter of helping their voice to be heard. Prayer in activism is also about attending to God's way of love not hate, respect not demonizing, gentleness not aggression.
- Work with others, people of good will, whether with a Christian faith or not, who share concern over the issue.
- Every context and every piece of activism is different because of the different circumstances in which they emerge. So each situation will need careful, wise research into the relevant decision-makers, influencers, allies, supporters, opponents. Sometimes getting the media – local, national, social – involved will be helpful; sometimes it will only antagonize and not help. Sometimes it can unfairly put someone in a spotlight they would not appreciate. In a campaign

for local sheltered accommodation, a central local campaigner didn't like the word 'activist' – so we didn't use it with her.

- Be aware of both the 'downstream' issue, helping a bullied asylum seeker, feeding the hungry with a foodbank, and the 'upstream' issue of government policy on asylum seekers, and of why people are having to go to foodbanks. Politics matters, and Jane has been campaigning hard alongside others against the social and economic injustices affecting our community, our city and beyond.

- 'If you have come here to help me, you are wasting my time, but if your liberation is bound up with mine, then let us work together' is a great quote from the indigenous Australian activist Lilla Watson. We are always learners, being ourselves liberated receivers as well as givers.

- Celebrate the victories: 'Phoenix from the Ashes', 'It took ten years', 'Congratulations to ...' were regularly on the front and inside pages of our community newspaper. Many get involved in their community and then drift away because of a disappointment, a misunderstanding, and their activist days are left behind. The story of Nehemiah, the story of a successful local campaign, the story of other campaigns in history, such as the Civil Rights battle or the apartheid struggle, can help us all to keep going as we feel part of a bigger picture where as activists we seek to make the world a better, fairer, more loving place.

Books to read

Ahern, Geoffrey, 1987, *Inner City God: The Nature of Belief in the Inner City*, London: Hodder & Stoughton.

Ballard, Paul; Pritchard, John, 1996, *Practical Theology in Action: Christian Thinking in the Service of Church and Society*, London: SPCK.

Hope, Anne; Timmel, Sally, 1967, *Training for Transformation: A Handbook for Community Workers*, Harare: Mambo Press.

Kelly, Kevin, 1992, *New Directions in Moral Theology*, London: Geoffrey Chapman.

King Jr, Martin Luther, 2001, *Strength to Love*, Minneapolis, MN: Fortress Press.

Sainsbury, Roger, 1970, *From a Mersey Wall*, London: Scripture Union.

Schluter, Michael; Ashcroft, John, 2005, *Jubilee Manifesto: A Framework, Agenda and Strategy for Christian Social Reform*, Leicester: IVP.

Sheppard, David; Worlock, Derek, 1988, *Better Together*, London: Hodder & Stoughton.

Useful website and report

The Langrove Action Story: www.togetherforthecommongood. co.uk/resources/research/articles/the-langrove-action-story. html.

Faith in the City: A Call for Action by Church and Nation: Report of the Archbishop of Canterbury's Commission on Urban Priority Areas, London: Church House Publishing, 1985.

Rule #6

Identify the Good Things and Give the Good Things Away

Things should belong to those who do well by them

One of my favourite plays is Bertolt Brecht's *The Caucasian Chalk Circle*. I will leave you to read, or even better, see the play for yourself. The play is about land rights, who the rightful owners of the land might be and who is best for it. It is about what justice looks like in complicated situations where ownership is contested, causes of oppression unclear and historical events make reconciliation seem impossible. The play starts with people in a commune fighting over who should work the land. They are waiting for an 'expert' to give judgement on their behalf. A storyteller arrives and offers to enact a play to help them with their decisions. The play within a play tells the story of Michael, a child born in great wealth as the governor's son, abandoned by his mother for the sake of a dress, and then brought up by a peasant girl called Grusha. Grusha protects, nourishes and lavishes kindness on Michael, she sacrifices love for him and she protects him in times of oppression. She describes her adopted child as a 'child of love'. When the child's birth mother claims him (in order to settle her inheritance), Grusha's love is tested in a court by Azdak, a drunken judge who appears to have no principles. The 'true mother' is asked to pull the child out of a hastily drawn chalk circle on the ground. The peasant mother refuses to do this for fear that the child be 'torn to pieces', but the governor's wife, the birth mother, grabs the child and claims her prize. When Azdak makes his judgement, he awards the child to the peasant mother: Grusha is the 'true mother'. The play within a play ends. We return to the storyteller in the epilogue, who bids us remember the wisdom of our elders: 'That what there is shall go to those who are good for it, Children to the motherly, that they prosper.' The storyteller goes on to talk about the ownership of both tools and land, pointing out that those who use them best reap the healthiest harvest.[1]

This chapter is about identifying the good things, discerning who is best for them and if necessary (if you are not best for them), being prepared to give those good things away. What we will explore here is what happens when we give away what is rightfully ours, when we allow others to flourish; what it feels like to let go of power, share glory, become generous and refuse to hold on to structures that prop us up but enslave others.

In November 2018, I was privileged to visit South Africa with Christian Aid alongside two other senior leaders from the Church of England and the Church of Ireland. As Christian Aid's Church Partnerships Manager, John Plant, explained: 'The purpose of the trip was for participants to explore the crucial role that church leaders can play in international development and to explore first hand the work of Christian Aid's global partners and the role that churches and church leaders are playing.'

Our host for the week was a project that Christian Aid supports – The Church Land Programme (CLP). This is an

1 Brecht, Bertolt, 2007 (1947), *The Caucasian Chalk Circle*, translated by Eric Bentley, London: Penguin Classics, p. 99.

independent non-profit organization that was initiated in 1996 as a joint project between the Association for Rural Advancement (Afra) and the Pietermaritzburg Agency for Christian Social Awareness (Pacsa), in response to the land reform process taking place in South Africa. It was established as an independent organization in 1997 and initially focused on church-owned land, while also challenging the Church to engage in the national land question and work for a just and sustainable agrarian transformation.

The CLP deals with real-life scenarios similar to the fictional one I described earlier in *The Caucasian Chalk Circle*. Their work is to help people discover who is best for the contested land; however, unlike the Brecht play, CLP does not act as judge in this process. Instead it works as an enabler: helping communities to uncover their own stories, revealing oppression and recovery, enabling them to determine future action, building up new patterns of restitution and restoration.

I have written some Bible thinking about generosity, and the story of the work of CLP will be told by the Director Graham Philpott and the CLP collective.

Generous act of giving

> Every generous act of giving, with every perfect gift, is from above, coming down from the Father of lights, with whom there is no variation or shadow due to change. (James 1.17)

Generosity is at the heart of the ministry and teaching of Jesus, and in this letter we read that the Church continued to grapple with generosity, goodness and social action. This letter attributed to James begins with a salutation that encourages the people of God to act with wisdom, to avoid careless doubt and pray for greater insight. The writer wants the reader to know that God is not interested in our attempts at striving for riches or in our busyness. God has no time for our excuses about life being a trial or our weak attempts at offering justification for giving in to temptation. The writer is very clear about what is at stake here. All good things come from God and the other stuff is just what happens because we exist – because we mess up, because life is life. Generosity is what God is. Even from the beginning of creation, our well-being and beauty has been God's enduring generous promise. As Paul Fromburg reminds us:

> Human beings are beautiful ... The whole history of our salvation rests on the claim that our value cannot be questioned. After their fall from grace, when God seeks after the first man and woman, it is not to destroy them but to clothe them. Our long walk back to Eden is on a pathway smoothed by God's love and mercy.[2]

So if God is generosity and Jesus embodied that generosity, what do we think we should dream to be? What is the Holy Spirit equipping us to live as? Well, I think we should dream to be generous people who aspire to work together to bring about love and mercy in the beautiful world God created for us to share!

Once James has clarified the situation about generosity, the letter goes on to say what this should look like. It asks the readers to be 'doers' – activists, to get on with activating the generosity plan. Being hearers is not enough; we need to get out there and do. The call to action is clear:

2 Fromberg, Paul, 2017, *The Art of Transformation: Three Things Churches do that Change Everything*, New York, Church Publishing, pp. 32–3.

But those who look into the perfect law, the law of liberty, and persevere, being not hearers who forget but doers who act – they will be blessed in their doing. If any think they are religious, and do not bridle their tongues but deceive their hearts, their religion is worthless. Religion that is pure and undefiled before God, the Father, is this: to care for orphans and widows in their distress, and to keep oneself unstained by the world. (James 1.25–27)

The difficult art of generosity is to be able to identify the gifts we possess – the assets we have to give. I don't just mean us personally, I mean 'us' in community. We individually have gifts but when they are put together they are multiplied by far more than their material assets alone. James wasn't writing to a person. This is a letter to a church, possibly a church with a bad reputation for action, or possibly James is attending to the error of overthinking and not getting on with things. Perhaps this church needed to rethink their vision and remember that they were there to put Jesus' plan into action and not just sit around talking about it.

Once we have collectively identified our assets, we need to find ways to generously give them away. Working our assets well is a real art and one that needs the wisdom James speaks of early in the letter. The stories of the way people and God have acted with generosity will inspire us, as will the rest of the letter. It goes on to warn against partiality – generosity needs to be indiscriminate. The letter explains that we are not saved by the doing: salvation is God's generous gift offered up by Jesus. Instead our activism, what James describes as 'works', is what enables us to become known as like God. Our communal Godlike work enacts salvation and brings hope to the world that needs to know where goodness, generosity, love, mercy and beauty come from. This letter is full of excellent teaching about how to live generously and carefully. I commend it to you.

On activism and generosity

Generous activism – this sounds like an attractive option, a worthwhile call to us all; a welcome respite in the midst of a capitalism that twists and distorts our humanity and our relations within the blessedness of this world. We seem to have entered into a pact in which our societies, our lives, our relations with each other and the non-human world, are structured on the basis of money, accumulation and profit. Generosity breaks with this pact; it names a different logic – a logic of giving, not denying. Surely such generous activism is to be welcomed and affirmed. Or is it? Is there a different experience of generosity? Is there a generosity that re-inscribes the dehumanizing pact?

The burn of a 'false generosity'

In John Steinbeck's seminal novel of the Great Depression, *The Grapes of Wrath* (1939), a character called Annie Little-field points to the humiliation of charity and the way it burns into the soul of a person forced to beg for help. With fierce eyes she says: 'We was hungry – they made us crawl for our dinner. They took our dignity. They – I hate 'em!' It is the indignity that beats people down, that steals hope and takes away humanity.[3]

---

3 Steinbeck, John, 2000 (1939), *The Grapes of Wrath*, London: Penguin, p. 331.

'They took our dignity'. It is not about their generosity, or what they gave, but more deeply about what they took – they took our dignity. Is it about how they gave, their stipulations, their intentions, the amount, the frequency, the condition-alities? Maybe – but more profoundly, it is about what they took – they took our dignity, and my man was beat. There is no generous activism here – just a man beaten and Annie Littlefield.

Beyond Annie Littlefield and her man, does this resonate? We hear so much from the resourced giver, the subject, but what of the targeted receiver, the object? We are grateful to Paulo Freire who, once again, helps us to see this in a systemic way and provides language that captures the harshness of it:

> Any attempt to 'soften' the power of the oppressor in defer-ence to the weakness of the oppressed almost always mani-fests itself in the form of false generosity; indeed, the attempt never goes beyond this. In order to have the continued opportunity to express their 'generosity', the oppressors must perpetuate injustice as well. An unjust social order is the permanent fount of this 'generosity', which is nourished by death, despair and poverty.[4]

This is harsh language that names this 'false generosity', but it is a generosity that is, unfortunately, the all too common experience in the world of activism. It is a generosity that 'makes a burn that don't come out'. We have professionalized this generosity and activism, and made it our business to be the subjects that set the trends, the methodologies, the indicators; and we have provided the labels for our objects (OVCs,

---

4 Freire, Paulo, 2000 (1970), *Pedagogy of the Oppressed*, New York: Bloomsbury Academic, p. 44.

beneficiaries), so that we/they are clear about their place in the world-as-it-is. Activism tends to assume that agency lies with groups of materially resourced and well-informed activists, acting and speaking for the causes and victims of our distorted society. Practices that proceed on these assumptions invariably reproduce the underlying architecture of practices and social relations that assault the dignity and very being of so many. Such a 'false generosity' perpetuates the fundamental injustice to which it is apparently responding. We have simply become much more organized in taking people's dignity.

This cannot be the generosity that faith communities – or any community – can be aligned with, a generosity and social order that is nourished by death, despair and poverty. We cannot enact a generosity that perpetuates the injustice to which it is responding. There is no place for an activism that uses the means of an unjust system and practice (a system of death, despair and poverty) to ameliorate the effects of that system, in the name of some greater end – it just leaves a lot of beaten people.

The possibility of a 'true generosity'

If this is Freire's 'false generosity', is there the possibility of a 'true generosity'? Maybe the possibility sits not in the shifting or repackaging or re-modelling of that which is given – but in the reclaiming of that which was taken. Annie Littlefield cries: 'They took our dignity.' Dignity! Maybe that is a better starting point, where the mutual recognition of dignities becomes the basis of a true generosity – a generosity predicated on egalitarianism; enacting a politics of dignity, now.

John Holloway, a contemporary thinker on a politics of

dignity, provides some helpful insights into the nature of this practice of dignity in a world that strips us of our humanity:

> Dignity is the immediate affirmation of negated subjectivity, the assertion, against a world that treats us as objects and denies our capacity to determine our own lives, that we are subjects capable and worthy of deciding for ourselves. Dignity in this sense means not only the assertion of our own dignity but also implies the recognition of the dignity of others. The 'other politics' [politics of dignity] means treating ourselves and others as doers, as subjects rather than objects, and finding appropriate forms of organisation to express this. In a world that constantly negates our dignity, this inevitably means a process of ever renewed exploration and creation of organisational forms.[5]

Within such a practice, acting out of this true generosity, justice is established when the logic of dignity and egalitarianism triumphs over the logic of the world-as-it-is. The logic of egalitarianism need not and should not be something we aim for – it's something we can and must do now, immediately, practically.

But generosity invariably assumes exactly the opposite. It takes the inequality of the world-as-it-is as given, and claims that social justice will come sometime in the future, after social change. And of course, it puts the power of agency in the hands of those with resources. The givers are the ones doing – the poor are reduced to objects of charity. That's simply never going to be the beginning of anything to do with actual justice – it simply and unavoidably re-inscribes the conditions of injustice; it takes our dignity.

---

5 Holloway, John, 2010, *Crack Capitalism*, London: Pluto Press, p. 39.

The love of people

It will be useful to return to Paulo Freire, as he was the one who named the problem of this 'false generosity'. Freire looks to the weakness of Annie Littlefield for hope and asserts:

> only power that springs from the weakness of the oppressed will be sufficiently strong to free both [the oppressed and the oppressor] ... True generosity consists precisely in fighting to destroy the causes which nourish false charity. False charity constrains the fearful and subdued, the 'rejects of life', to extend their trembling hands.[6]

This 'true generosity' takes us to the root of our activism – the love of people; a love that fights to destroy the causes of death, poverty, dehumanizing wealth; a love that longs to make poverty impossible; a love that acts to end the cycles of death and indignity. We cannot have a 'love-of-the-people-activism' without having dignity as the basis of our practice:

- an activism of doers – seeing people as subjects not objects;
- an activism that abandons the assumption that it is the agency of the powerful that matters;
- a generous activism that is based in the hands and minds of people who have nothing, the power that springs from the weakness of the oppressed;
- a generous activism that explores and creates organizational forms that express and affirm our dignity.

---

6 Freire, *Pedagogy of the Oppressed*, chapter 1.

RULE #6: GIVE THE GOOD THINGS AWAY

Principles of good stuff

At the Church Land Programme (CLP), as we have explored a practice of solidarity and dignity, we have reflected on the practical outworking of a 'love of the people' for our collective praxis. We have named for ourselves some principles of good practice, a practice that assumes that the people who are affected are the agents of human liberation. Such a praxis implies a faith in the struggles of the people, and cannot continue the myth that some other power or agent (let alone our small organization) can 'deliver' real change and freedom, no matter how generous we are. However, that faith is not a blind faith that romanticizes 'the people' or assumes every grass-roots action to be emancipatory. It is possible – indeed necessary – to make principled judgements around these questions and to begin to discern a generous doing based on the mutual recognition of dignities. The following are principles that have emerged out of our praxis, naming the doing that we are seeking to support and learn from:

- It is action that arises when those whom we are told 'do not count' actually make themselves count. It is the speaking of those who have been told to be silent. It is the thinking of those who are not supposed to think.
- It emerges from, and proceeds within, a radical democratic base. This is not about a liberal representative democracy, but about ongoing practice that is based on the assumption that everybody matters, here and now. This means that egalitarianism is axiomatic and is practised consistently.
- It is action that makes universal truth claims. People's specific actions make claims that are true for everyone, everywhere in and of this world. It cannot be true for only a certain class, gender, race or nation. It is action that

makes claims that are true for our whole world, including the non-human world.

- It is a generosity that is announced/made in 'out-of-order' actions. These are actions that do not perpetuate the world-as-it-is, but open paths for the world that is emerging.

At CLP we talk about these as the 'principles of good stuff', features of what we discern to be a generous activism that fights against death, despair and poverty, destroying the causes of a false charity.

If the mutual recognition of dignities becomes the basis of our practice of generosity, then we begin making new paths opened by our mutual doing, we move forward together as subjects not objects. We explore and create organizational forms that express and affirm our dignity, and we make the world anew in the hands and minds of people who have 'nothing' but the enormous power and creativity of our human capacities. In the doing, we make and discover emerging cracks in the world-as-it-is, spaces and moments in which we assert a different type of doing, based not on profit and power-over but on freely choosing how to expend our power-to. These are cracks that are explorations in a politics of dignity; cracks of generosity founded on our mutual recognition of dignities.

Tools for the toolkit

In considering some tips for practice, what we can offer is a 'confession of faith', which we generated regarding what we believe about a praxis of dignity. It is a statement that emerged in the midst of our journey to remain true to an emancipatory praxis in our context.

We believe/We no longer doubt for a second:

- That people demonstrate their sovereignty through the struggles they lead.
- That we are not alone – and that the more our praxis is connected to popular and genuine rebellion, the less alone we are, and the more ordinary and democratic the struggle becomes.
- That things happen beyond our control and our effort, and beyond our resources and words.
- That faith in truth keeps us going on an uncertain path – and sometimes a messy ride.
- That love, respect and fidelity are key: love of the people; respect because everyone matters really and we express this in our action and listening; fidelity in being true.
- Our faith is a praxis that places us against the world-as-it-is.
- That thought, especially collective processes of thinking, are key to liberatory action.
- That liberation of the poor and the oppressed is liberation of everyone.

Books to read

Alker, Adrian, 2016, *Is A Radical Church Possible?*, Alresford: Christian Alternative Books.

Annan, Kent, 2016, *Slow Kingdom Coming: Practices for Doing Justice, Loving Mercy and Walking Humbly in the World*, Downers Grove, IL: IVP.

Bauckham, Richard, 2003, *Bible and Mission: Christian Witness in a Postmodern World*, Milton Keynes: Paternoster Press.

Boff, Leonardo; Boff, Clodovis, 1987, *Introducing Liberation Theology*, Tunbridge Wells: Burns & Oates/Search Press.

Brueggemann, Walter, 2014, *Sabbath as Resistance: Saying No to the Culture of Now*, Louisville, KY: Westminster John Knox Press.

Freire, Paulo, 2000 (1970), *Pedagogy of the Oppressed*, New York: Bloomsbury Academic.

Gutiérrez, Gustavo, 1973, *A Theology of Liberation*, London: SCM Press.

Howson, Chris, 2011, *A Just Church: 21st Century Liberation Theology in Action*, London: Continuum.

Lane, Chris, 2017, *Ordinary Miracles: Mess, Meals and Meeting Jesus in Unexpected Places*, Watford: Instant Apostle.

Useful websites

Christian Aid, www.christianaid.org.uk/.
Church Land Programme, www.churchland.org.za/.

Rule #7

Diversify

One body many parts

We are learning that people worship in different ways; we are starting to understand that we like to mix things up a bit and need to explore alternative ways of being in community. As the people of God we are called to be one body, but we are not called to be the same part. Our diversity is what makes us who we are, and who we are is loved by God.

Jesus prayed for those who believe in and follow him, 'that they all may be one' (John 17.21). Thank God he didn't say 'one and the same!'

The educational charity Inclusive Church has produced an excellent four-session course called 'Radical Welcome', aimed at helping churches begin to look at what it might mean to go beyond being inclusive – to be radically welcoming of diversity.[1] The third session invites us to reflect on the journey, from inviting, through inclusion, to radical welcome. Simply, the message of a culture of invitation is 'Come, join our community and share our cultural heritage'; in other words, 'Come and be like us.' Inclusion means 'Help us to be diverse', while radical welcome means 'Bring your culture, your voice, your whole self – we want to engage in truly mutual relationship.'

---

1 See www.inclusive-church.org/resources/radical-welcome-course.

This chapter has been written by Kieran Bohan, Open Table network coordinator, and his husband Warren Hartley, LGBTQIA+ Ministry Facilitator at St Bride's Liverpool, home of the first Open Table community. They have collaborated to write the Bible thinking, the case study and their tips. What follows is their reflection on seeking to offer radical welcome to people of diverse gender identities and sexual orientations through the Open Table network of ecumenical worship communities. Open Table believe these basic principles are good practice for any Christian community that is serious about embracing and celebrating the full diversity of humanity.

The mustard seed

The kingdom of heaven is like a mustard seed that some-one took and sowed in his field; it is the smallest of all the seeds, but when it has grown it is the greatest of shrubs and becomes a tree, so that the birds of the air come and make nests in its branches. (Matthew 13.31–32)

This parable is one of the shorter parables of Jesus. The plant it refers to is generally considered to be black mustard, a large annual plant up to 9 feet (2.7 metres) tall, but growing from a small seed (this smallness is also used as a symbol of faith in Matthew 17.20 and Luke 17.6).

The parable suggests the growth of the kingdom of God from tiny beginnings. The one sowing the seed may represent Jesus, and the plant may be a symbol of the kingdom of God. The nesting birds recall Old Testament texts that emphasize the diversity, abundance and universal reach of God's kingdom:

Its leaves were beautiful, its fruit abundant, and on it was food for all. Under it the wild animals found shelter, and the birds lived in its branches; from it every creature was fed. (Daniel 4.12 NIV)

However, a real mustard plant is unlikely to attract nesting birds, so Jesus seems deliberately to emphasize astonishing extravagance in his analogy. Some commentators have suggested that the birds represent Gentiles seeking refuge with Israel, or the 'sinners' with whom Jesus was criticized for associating.

Some have identified a 'subversive and scandalous' element to this parable – the fast-growing nature of the mustard plant makes it a 'weed' with 'dangerous takeover properties'.[2]

Pliny the Elder, in his *Natural History* (published around AD 78) wrote that: 'mustard ... is extremely beneficial for the health. It grows entirely wild ... when it has once been sown it is scarcely possible to get the place free of it.'[3] Jesus could have spoken of a genuine tree but, in the words of the American New Testament scholar Ben Witherington, the mustard plant demonstrates that:

Though the dominion appeared small like a seed during Jesus' ministry, it would inexorably grow into something large and firmly rooted, which some would find shelter in and others would find obnoxious and try to root out.[4]

Not only that: when Jesus says, 'The kingdom of heaven is like a mustard seed that someone took and sowed in his field',

---

2 Crossan, John Dominic, 1991, *The Historical Jesus*, New York: HarperCollins, p. 279.

3 Pliny the Elder, *Natural History*, translated by Harris Rackham, Loeb, 1950, Book XIX, Chapter LIV.

4 Witherington, Ben, 2001, *The Gospel of Mark: A Socio-rhetorical Commentary*, Grand Rapids, MI: Eerdmans, pp. 171–2.

he may be deliberately provoking the anxiety of his listeners. Jesus would have known that when they heard these words, the laws of Leviticus would come to mind that forbid planting more than one type of seed in a field, which the book of Leviticus calls 'an abomination'. The shock of this image for Jesus' listeners would be like Jesus saying to us, 'The kingdom of God is like a child who took a handful of dandelion seeds and sowed them in your lettuce patch'![5]

Open Table is an ecumenical Christian worship community that offers a warm welcome to people who are Lesbian, Gay, Bisexual, Transgender, Queer/Questioning, Intersex, Asexual (LGBTQIA) and all who seek an inclusive Church.

We share this reflection on the parable of the mustard seed, as a metaphor for the extraordinary growth of Open Table, with those who are exploring whether this ministry will enable their own communities to be more welcoming of diversity.

Come as you are

Open Table began at St Bride's Liverpool in June 2008, meeting once a month for a communion service. At the first planning meeting, someone said: 'Will it be "open table"?' When she explained that it means all are welcome, all can come as they are, we felt this was so important because we heard too many stories of people who feared exclusion, or were excluded, from their church community, who felt unheard or unable to express themselves or give their talents. So Open Table was born. Now Open Table communities

---

5 Reverend Laurie DeMott, 2019, 'The Mustard Seed', Union University Church, 17 February, www.unionuniversitychurch.org/2019/02/17/the-mustard-seed (accessed 11 September 2019).

gather across the UK, hosted by inclusive churches, serving more than 300 people each month.

As we write, Open Table is now in its twelfth year – when we first gathered in June 2008, as half a dozen supporters of Changing Attitude, which campaigned for LGBTI inclusion in the Church of England, we couldn't have dreamed that in 2019 we would be heading towards 20 Open Table communities across England and Wales. More than 80 other churches have also contacted us to explore bringing this expression of the abundance of God's love and outrageous hospitality to their church and community. Most of these churches have made first contact since February 2017, when the Archbishop of Canterbury called for a 'radical new Christian inclusion' following the Church of England General Synod's rejection of the House of Bishops' report on marriage and same-sex relationships:

> The way forward needs to be about love, joy and celebration of our humanity; of our creation in the image of God, of our belonging to Christ – all of us, without exception, without exclusion.[6]

Like the mustard seed, Open Table's growth has been both wild and, we hope, beneficial – it has provided shelter for those on the edges of our Christian traditions, like those with whom Jesus was criticized for associating by the religious authorities of his day. Some see it as subversive and scandalous and would want to root it out, and some even see us as 'an abomination'. As we reflect on our growth as a diverse and

---

6 Archbishop Justin Welby, 2017, 'Statement from the Archbishop of Canterbury following today's General Synod', 15 February, www.archbishopofcanterbury.org/speaking-and-writing/speeches/statement-archbishop-canterbury-following-todays-general-synod (accessed 11 September 2019).

dispersed community, we pray for the courage, the creativity and the clarity to see it grow into something large and firmly rooted – a true image of the kingdom of God here among us.

Our primary goal is to explore faith for LGBTQIA+ Christians, and assist one another in integrating our spiritual and sexual or gender identities, as for some these have been in direct conflict. We also welcome and affirm family members, friends and all who also seek an inclusive church. We do this by creating safe sacred space, with a real sense of God's presence, where we can bring all of ourselves to God and to each other, where we can invite everyone without exception to 'come as you are'.

We express this most simply in hospitality – we host the Open Table community rather than lead or run it.

> The real host is the one who offers that space where we do not have to be afraid and where we can listen to our own inner voices and find our own personal way of being human.[7]

This is both simple and radical. It is a ministry of presence – visible, counter-cultural and hard work – which can give a real taste of the kingdom. It isn't about campaigning, but it can bring external change through non-violent resistance to unjust structures in the Church.

Since 2015 (as Open Table has multiplied and spread across diocesan, denominational and regional boundaries), we have consulted with all the active and emerging Open Table communities to produce a statement of the shared requirements and recommendations, mission, vision and values of the Open Table network. Each Open Table worshipping community, though in diverse host churches and locations, shares these

---

7 Nouwen, Henri, 1996, *Reaching Out*, London: Fount, p. 74.

core intentions so people know that each and every Open Table community is a 'safe-enough' sacred place where all are free to 'come as you are'.

Each Open Table community is independent, but we offer mutual support, encouragement and learning from our experience. To be an Open Table community, there are four requirements: first, come and see what we do at our gatherings in Liverpool. If there is one nearer to you, you'd be welcome to visit one of the other Open Table communities (though bear in mind that they are at an earlier stage of development). Second, take it to your church leadership to pass a resolution to ensure support, safeguarding and accountability. Third, Open Table is at heart a worshipping community with a eucharistic focus, hence the name – Open Table = open communion for all. Other activities are encouraged, as long as the main regular activity has this focus; that is, a communion service or *agape* meal. Finally, in the planning and practice of liturgy and related activities, we encourage a grass-roots approach where possible, enabling LGBTQIA+ people to be heard, to contribute, to serve one another in a community of integrity and equity.

We also recommend that, to help promote inclusive ministry and community, a church seeking to host an Open Table community becomes a member of Inclusive Church[8] and registers the church as a Visible Congregation and the Open Table worship community as a Visible Gathering with OneBodyOneFaith (formerly the Lesbian and Gay Christian Movement).[9] We also recommend that the church community signs the Open Church Charter and becomes part of the Oasis Charitable Trust's Open Church Network.[10] Working

---

8 www.inclusive-church.org/join-inclusive-church.

9 www.onebodyonefaith.org.uk/about-us/get-visible.

10 www.openchurch.network/content/sign-open-church-charter.

in collaboration and solidarity with these organizations offers churches strength and support as well as a shared language and mission.

The Open Table mission is to create safe sacred spaces for all people to encounter the infinite, unconditional, intimate love of God, offering a warm welcome to all who identify as Lesbian, Gay, Bisexual, Transgender, Queer/Questioning, Intersex, Asexual (LGBTQIA), their family and friends, and all who seek an inclusive church. We believe our lives, our identities and our relationships are precious gifts from God that we are called to live out with integrity. Our desire is to continue to build a community where this is evident, and which equips others to go out and do the same.

Our values are integral to the way we live in community and enable us to inhabit our social space. We expect all Open Table congregations to be:

- Safe: Support, accountability, safeguarding training for leaders.
- Sacred: Meeting God and each other on holy ground through heartfelt liturgy and music.
- Sacramental: Worship as holy hospitality celebrated in Communion.
- Sustainable: Consistent, for the long term, committed to sharing learning.
- Space: Welcoming, inclusive, accessible.

The way of offering hospitality we have embedded in the life of Open Table is known as the 'person-centred approach'. This follows the teaching of Dr Carl Rogers, who emphasized the quality of relationship and a person's ability to discover within themselves the resources for personal growth and fulfilment, as in the words of Jesus: 'I came that they may have life, and have it abundantly' (John 10.10).

Carl Rogers began training for Christian ministry but gave this up and went on to become one of the most influential figures in twentieth-century psychology. Brian Thorne, a former lecturer in Psychology at Norwich University and a committed Anglican, is perhaps the best-known British writer on this approach. In his 2003 book *Infinitely Beloved: The Challenge of Divine Intimacy*, he described being person-centred as forming relationships where people can feel safe enough to face their pain and increase their awareness of themselves and others. This practice enhances self-confidence and self-worth so that participants feel genuinely accepted and understood and begin to reveal the wonder of their own natures. By engaging in this practice and living these ideas out in community, participants can become more self-accepting, more responsive to others and better able to harness their gifts and abilities in the service of the wider community.[11]

It is important to note that this isn't something that someone does to another – it is about creating relationships where both parties grow, which require three 'core conditions'. First, unconditional positive regard – non-judgmental warmth and acceptance. Second, empathy – 'walking in someone else's shoes'; more than sympathy, it is a compassionate response that promotes connection between equals. Third, congruence – being genuine, real, authentic, honest.

So how does this all work in practice? We've shared theological reflection and a case study from the particular community of which we are privileged to be a part, but what about wider application? Through applying the rule of diversity and reflecting on the practice of Open Table, our three steps for activism are: BE, CREATE, ACT.

---

11 Thorne, Brian, 2003, *Infinitely Beloved: The Challenge of Divine Intimacy*, London: Darton, Longman and Todd.

Our first step is to BE a host of diversity. As the mustard tree provides shelter, so an effective activist creates spaces and relationships that host diversity. Hospitality is at the very heart of everything we do. While we work with LGBTQIA+ communities, all are welcome. Don't just gather like-minded people together, just gather people together! It will be untidy, unwieldy and like herding cats, but keep hosting, inviting and showing up, even when it's tough. Each person will have unique gifts and needs, and all that wisdom will make a difference to your action. Start where you are, and with what have you have, even if it is just 'the smallest of seeds'.

This leads us to our second step for activism: we aim to CREATE communities and relationships that offer the core conditions and values we inhabit. We believe this is the work of building the kingdom (or kin-dom) of God. Key to this is 'unconditional positive regard' – every human being without exception is a child of God. Treat them as such, expressed in how you invite, welcome and offer hospitality:

> I've learned that people will forget what you said, people will forget what you did, but people will never forget how you made them feel.[12]

Empathy is also a core condition of the person-centred approach to the creation of community. Empathy helps us to learn from the experience of others, really listen to people's stories, and expand your collective knowledge of the breadth and diversity of experience among the members of your community and beyond.

Creating a community where each person can be genuine and authentic doesn't mean 'anything goes'. Congruence is

---

12 Carl W. Buehner, cited by Richard L. Evans, 1971, *Richard Evans' Quote Book*, Salt Lake City, UT: Publishers Press, p. 244.

vital to the way we create community and as such compromise and empathy are needed. It does not deny that difference exists. Unity implies that there is difference, otherwise we would have uniformity. We'd much rather see a colourful and diverse unity than a colourless, bland uniformity! You don't all even need to agree, but congruence is about remaining in relationship with empathy and unconditional positive regard. Congruence is also challenging behaviour that stops others in the community from experiencing the core conditions. Through this experience you, and those around you, will grow and transform to become like the mustard tree 'so that the birds of the air come and make nests in its branches'.

Our third step is ACT by being visible and present. This is about being real and authentic – it's where the change of activism occurs. But you can't get to step three without taking steps one and two. The first two do the hard work of creating the foundations of your work beyond your own community. Interestingly, by valuing diversity and creating a community, you are already being an activist, so the step of acting becomes a natural and organic outworking of the community and relationships. Indeed, you can't help but overflow. It also roots your work, so that even if someone attempts to remove it, like the mustard seed it will just keep on returning.

To be an activist, you can't just jump in the deep end – if you do, you run the risk of simply splashing around and making no lasting difference, or worse, hurting already hurt people. By doing the work of creating space in which each person can heal and be healed, your activism is rooted and considered. As Richard Rohr reminds us: 'If you do not transform your pain, you will always transmit it.'[13]

---

13 Rohr, Richard, 2014, *A Lever and a Place to Stand: The Contemplative Stance, the Active Prayer*, Mahwah, NJ: Paulist Press, p. 103.

By co-creating community, you and others can transform your pain (individually and collectively), so that your activism doesn't become about transmitting it but rather transforming the source of the pain.

Our Open Table slogan #ComeAsYouAre reminds us as we meet that we come together in community 'as we are' – loved by God and cherished by those who gather in the name of Christ. John Bell has inspired us with this call to action: 'Those of us who … know the Love of God cannot stay silent!'[14]

So be courageous. Having known the love of God, you cannot stay silent! Imagine what it would be like to be a part of a church community that attempted to live out this approach.[15]

Tools for the toolkit

- Be a host who welcomes diversity.
- Create a community that fosters relationships that offer the Core Conditions: Unconditional Positive Regard, Empathy and Congruence/Authenticity.
- Root your activism in being visible and present within the community you are serving and in the context you wish to see changed.
- Be persistent! Don't give up, particularly when it hurts. But do listen to the pain to see what it might be teaching you.

---

14 Bell, John, 'Rampant Heterosexualism', Greenbelt Festival August 2017: www.greenbelt.org.uk/talks/rampant-heterosexualism.

15 To find out where and when you can #ComeAsYouAre, visit www.opentable.lgbt.

- Don't be afraid of difference – be prepared to be changed by the people you encounter.
- Be aware that you will get it wrong, and often. Keep trying, keep learning and be prepared to say sorry … lots!
- Start where you are and with what you have. Don't wait until you have it all together, otherwise you'll never get started.
- Question everything. Don't just do something because 'that's why you do it' or 'that is what churches do'. Do everything you do with a reason and be prepared to change your mind.
- Remember whose kingdom you're building! Share leadership with diverse, rich, gathered wisdom. It stops your activism being all about you. It is humbling yet empowering.
- Don't forget to enjoy the ride or stop and smell the roses along the way. It will remind you why you do the work you do and keep you motivated.

Books to read

Bayes, Paul, 2019, *The Table: Knowing Jesus: Prayer, Friendship, Justice*, London: Darton, Longman and Todd.

Beeching, Vicky, 2017, *Undivided: Coming Out, Becoming Whole, and Living Free From Shame*, London: Collins.

Edman, Liz, 2017, *Queer Virtue: What LGBTQ People Know about Life and Love and How It Can Revitalize Christianity*, Boston, MA: Beacon Press.

Fromberg, Paul, 2017, *The Art Of Transformation: Three Things Churches do that Change Everything*, New York: Church Publishing.

Greenough, Chris, 2019, *Queer Theologies: The Basics*, London: Routledge.

Higgins, Gregory C., 2009, *Wrestling with the Questions: An Introduction to Contemporary Theologies*, Minneapolis, MN: Fortress Press.

Ozanne, Jayne, 2016, *Journeys in Grace and Truth: Revisiting Scripture and Sexuality*, London: Ekklesia.

Rohr, Richard, 2019, *The Universal Christ: How a Forgotten Reality Can Change Everything We See, Hope For and Believe*, London: SPCK.

Useful websites

Inclusive Church, www.inclusive-church.org.
Open Table, http://opentable.lgbt/.

Rule #8

Make it Count

People on purpose

It might surprise you that I have included counting and measuring as a rule. A few years back I would have argued against the need for Impact Measuring Tools and so on. I would have seen any such forms of evaluation as over-bureaucratic, time wasting and an unnecessary distraction from the 'real work' of being an activist. But I have started to realize that I have no idea about the impact of much of my pre-counting activism. Because I didn't evaluate, I can only speculate; I can't give you any detail of the long-term impact of interventions or plan future endeavours based on previous success. I don't have an accurate idea about how to replicate this work and can only tell you my opinions because I didn't gather the thoughts and experiences of others. As soon as I started to make social action count I started to understand how to focus, how to be more accurate; I wasted less time and felt that I was going to projects better prepared. It has helped to do better handover of work, and saved on replication.

I and my collaborator on this chapter, the Christian-activist-researcher Dr Naomi Maynard, share similar concerns about the measuring and counting of social action.

Naomi writes:

Why do we count, measure, evaluate? Doesn't it distract from 'doing'? It takes time, energy, planning when we could be loving, feeding, sharing, caring.

Improve, expand, grow, be bigger, better, do more for less, be more efficient, more effective. This is the chant of neoliberalism, creeping into (and slowly strangling) our third sector. Do we, as Christians, want to dance to this beat?

Our God sees what is done in the quiet, God is there in those small acts of kindness, God loves the local warrior diligently working away, transforming lives. So why do we need to shout about it? Should we?

These are the voices I hear and the tensions I am holding, wrestling with as I write. They lurk in among these reflections.

I asked Naomi to collaborate on this chapter because she is very good at counting, measuring and telling the stories of the impact of the work of the people of God. Naomi currently works for Church Army as a researcher and is the Project Development Lead Officer for the CUF and Diocese of Liverpool joint venture, Together Liverpool. Naomi and I have worked together on a number of projects and we are keen to find straightforward ways to measure the impact of Christian activism. We want to enable churches and communities to focus on present needs, identify current resources, seek God's blessing of the endeavour, share whatever is available, and then gauge the impact of the intervention. We believe that social action is the good news of the glory of God and as such will enable our church communities to grow and flourish. By making this work count, making sure we understand the impact, we think we are being people of purpose, keeping to our goals and trying to remain focused on our outcomes (while not missing the accidental snippets of random glory!).

I have written the Bible thinking and Naomi has drawn from her experience as a researcher to write the case study. We are grateful to Heather Buckingham at the Trussell Trust and Hannah Rich from Theos for their contributions to this chapter.

One Messiah, 5000 men (and an unknown number of women and children), some disciples, five loaves, two fish and 12 baskets of leftovers

> Now when Jesus heard this, he withdrew from there in a boat to a deserted place by himself. But when the crowds heard it, they followed him on foot from the towns. When he went ashore, he saw a great crowd; and he had compassion for them and cured their sick. When it was evening, the disciples came to him and said, 'This is a deserted place, and the hour is now late; send the crowds away so that they may go into the villages and buy food for themselves.' Jesus said to them, 'They need not go away; you give them something to eat.' They replied, 'We have nothing here but five loaves and two fish.' And he said, 'Bring them here to me.' Then he ordered the crowds to sit down on the grass. Taking the five loaves and the two fish, he looked up to heaven, and blessed and broke the loaves, and gave them to the disciples, and the disciples gave them to the crowds. And all ate and were filled; and they took up what was left over of the broken pieces, twelve baskets full. And those who ate were about five thousand men, besides women and children. (Matthew 14.13–21)

Just to place this story in context: at the beginning of this chapter we read that Herod has arrested and senselessly murdered

John the Baptist – Jesus' pathfinder, messenger, cousin, friend – decapitated for the sake of a party favour! This passage we have read is offered with the cloud of mourning around it. The story begins with the sad words: 'Now when Jesus heard this, he withdrew from there in a boat to a deserted place by himself. But when the crowds heard it, they followed him on foot from the towns.' In this context – we are told – Jesus 'felt sorry for them and healed everyone who was sick'.

Grief and a thwarted attempt at alone time: Jesus has compassion. Jesus heals.

And here begins the story of the feeding of the 5,000 – a story of bad preparation, emptiness, a desert place, of not enough, which is broken and shared out, of blessing and abundance; a story where counting matters and injustice is noted, where there wasn't enough but there is plenty left over. It is an impossible story. But it is a story that I can retell week in week out – a story of our foodbank and our volunteer programme, a story of risk and despair being opened out into opportunity and hope.

Those people that Jesus felt sorry for, these were people with needs – so many needs that they gathered and waited, they risked their time and they stayed even though they had nothing – and for whatever reason, they came to Jesus to have their needs met. They wanted healing, they wanted to be near him; and there were a lot of them. Indeed, the writer notes that there were 5,000 men – and he notes his own prejudice in that he doesn't count women and children (so given the demographic of current church attendance, we can assume 15,000 women and 10,000 children – 30,000 altogether). Suddenly the problems associated with lack of accurate counting become apparent! Whatever, let's just understand that there were a lot of people.

So the disciple's observation that the place that had been a space for healing had become a desert with no facilities and no food was not unreasonable. Sending the crowd home was a sensible move. And Jesus' command to feed them is absurd, particularly in the light of the rations available – just five loaves and two fish.

Each week our local food bank (read about this food bank in Rule #2: Be Useful) faces the same problem – there's not enough. Every week thousands of people across our country face the same problem – there's not enough. What do we do? Give up, face reality, send people away?

The truth is that those people were the responsibility of the disciples; they were the presenting problem in the moment. Jesus expected them to take responsibility for the situation. And they do. They create a system, get them sat down and give Jesus the meagre rations.

Jesus breaks the bread, gives thanks and then asks his disciples to distribute it.

We only have what we have; we can't offer more than we have. Some of us might be able to offer more, but most of us don't have many extra supplies. We can only operate from our assets. There's no point worrying about what we don't have, that doesn't exist. This is the place to start. This is the point from which to begin being generous. Give it up. Don't withhold.

Once the asset is identified, offer it freely, offer it sacramentally: give thanks, ask for blessing on it, then get on with it. Share it. Liberally.

In Jesus' story we are told that everyone (all 30,000 people or thereabouts) were fed, and there was a lot left over (12 large baskets – seems they could be more accurate with the counting of food than with people). This story is a story of asset, sacrifice, thanksgiving and abundance. It's an impossible story. But then aren't so many of our stories impossible?

My observation is that the solution to need is both utterly straightforward and totally complicated. The problem of solving the injustice of national and international poverty is massive – as individuals we can do nothing that will have any significant impact. Yet we can attend to the immediate concerns that present themselves to us in the here and now. Jesus was dealing with the systemic issues of the massive political and religious injustices the people faced. His very existence threatened the occupying forces. The gospels are full of stories of his railing against the authorities, lawyers and those who lied to the people. But this did not blind him to the need of the people in the moment. Those people needed feeding. There and then. And it was his responsibility to provide – as part of his response to the complex needs of the people.

The complexity of the task we face is that we have to respond to human need (without exception – we don't get to choose who to help or not to help); we are also called to challenge injustice; we are required to care for the earth; proclaim God's kingdom; and teach, baptize and nurture faith. This is the mission of the Church. This is the mission of God's people – each of us. But we need to work out of our assets – from what we have. This is all we can do – offer it up to Jesus, expect it to be broken and blessed, then start handing it out. Morsel by morsel.

Measuring our social action

Naomi says:
Over the last decade I have identified as a Christian-activist-researcher, adopting the labels separately at first and increasingly now together.

For many years I found being a Christian an unsettling

label; my faith – and how I acted it out, in small ways, through love and friendships and service – did not seem to measure up to the loud expressions and emotions of those around me. I felt most 'me' (the 'me' I see now that God had lovingly created) in my work as a social researcher, exploring questions of faith, justice and poverty. Feeling a sense of guilt that this wasn't how I felt on Sundays, in my initial years as a researcher I clung on to a phrase I had heard years ago about doing everything with excellence as if doing it for God.

Activism wasn't something I used to think much about. It was placards and sit-ins. Activists were 'out there', doing extraordinary things. Not me. This changed while conducting my doctoral research about children's rights activists. Listening to the stories of young adults reflecting back on their teenage years spent engaging with participatory activist organizations, I could see that the outworkings of this time often now materialized in their everyday actions that challenged and disrupted how children were positioned in society. Activism was not an 'add on' to their lives at home or work, it was an embedded way of being, a driving desire to see change that infiltrates how we act and think in the everyday spaces we are in.

Through this realization, alongside the wise encouragements of others, and a growing confidence that God made us all with different ways to interact with him and his world, I have come to see my faith and my activist heart to challenge injustice not as an add on to my work, but an integral part of it – regardless of the subject I am studying. This heart influences the projects I engage with, the approaches I take and the way I write. In turn these projects spill over into my beyond-work life, the stories of poverty and injustice I hear through work playing no small part in why my family now lives and worships in what the Church of England terms an Urban Priority Area, in the Diocese of Liverpool.

This rule for Christian activists encourages us to care about numbers. A brief look at the website of the Research and Statistics Unit of the Church of England will tell you that the Church of England is, in many ways, already good at counting. We count our money, our attendance, even our choirs. National newspapers publish a now nearly annual lament about falling numbers, closing churches (often missing the moments of celebration as the Church morphs into new spaces, reaching new demographics in new ways). But what about the ways we are church beyond Sundays? The Knit and Natter gatherings fighting social isolation, the support groups for those struggling with addiction, the youth clubs open among a sea of cuts, the inner-city churchyard lovingly tended so that commuters get a reminder of God's creation, the late-night food parcels given from our food banks, food pantries or from the vicarage door? How do we count those moments, big and small, when we are the hands and feet of Jesus? Should we count them? How does this relate to those troubling attendance numbers?

These are the questions the Church of England is beginning to ask through the GRA:CE project[1] and ones we have started to explore in the Diocese of Liverpool.[2]

---

1 www.theosthinktank.co.uk/research/2000/01/31/the-grace-project.

2 https://churcharmy.org/Articles/532825/What_we_do/Research_Unit/A_Bigger_Difference.aspx.

GRA:CE Project

The GRA:CE Project is a three-year research project in partnership between Theos and Church Urban Fund, exploring the connections between church growth, social action and discipleship in the Church of England.

- How are growing churches engaging with social issues?
- Does social action help churches grow?
- Do people grow as disciples as they connect with others through social action?

The GRA:CE Project is exploring these questions, and more, through a three-year programme of both qualitative and quantitative research. It aims to provide an enriching combination of learning, challenge, and encouragement, opening up fresh conversations about what it means for churches to seek fullness of life for our communities and society at a time of socio-economic change and uncertainty.

Telling our story

Bigger difference: social action and church growth in the Diocese of Liverpool

In 2017, churches were asked about their social action in their Statistics for Mission return. The diocese commissioned Church Army's Research Unit to analyse this data and speak to church leaders and parishioners about how social action relates to church growth and discipleship.

We found that:

- Churches across the diocese were involved in a wide range of social action activities. They were running and hosting social action activities, either alone or in partnership with other community organizations and faith groups.
- Churches' involvement in social action was motivated by four overlapping reasons: to serve the community; to tell people about God; to address an injustice; to get people into church.
- Social action can lead to numerical church growth, and the development of new congregations. It can also lead to spiritual church growth: as parishioners' faith is stretched, challenged and encouraged through connecting with their communities.

We learnt that:

- The definition of social action on the ground was much broader than the one offered in Statistics for Mission. Social action is more than regular, church-based activities – it is also those one-off community events, the generous use of the church's assets and resources, our involvement in local and national politics and the small unseen neighbourly acts.
- The five marks of mission were a useful tool to stimulate discussions about how faith connects with social action.

We reflected that:

- The impact of social action activities on church growth may be small-scale, slow and difficult to accurately ascertain. Churches may only engage with people once, never knowing the impact of that interaction.
- There is space for encouragement: large numbers of people are brought into contact with Christians each week through social action activities. Here they encounter Jesus through his people.

These projects start to shed light on a different truth about the Church, one step removed from the powerful (at times crippling) discourse of decline. They point to a Church that has quietly, humbly stepped in and stepped up as the state has withdrawn. They begin to show how social action overlaps with church growth, evangelism and discipleship, how it is central to faith: demanding attention from church decision-makers.

Data on churches and social action

We asked Heather Buckingham about the nature of the data on the impact of social action. She told us this:
It is a bit of a paradox that even as numbers attending weekly religious services or meetings have fallen over the past decade, churches' responses to social issues in communities have become more visible.[3] Most prominent in the public sphere in recent years have been food banks, owing in part to their

3 NatCen (2017) British Social Attitudes Survey, www.bsa. natcen.ac.uk/latest-report/british-social-attitudes-28/religion.aspx.

rapid spread as well as to the Trussell Trust's effective coordination and communication of data and stories about their use. Research conducted by the Church of England in 2017 found that over 60 per cent of Anglican churches support a food bank in some way, whether by providing donations of food, volunteers, a venue or in other ways.[4] Food banks have also seen local churches of different denominations partnering together in new ways, with Anglicans, Baptists, Catholics, Pentecostals, Independent Evangelicals, Presbyterians, Methodists and other denominations all involved, alongside many volunteers of no religious faith and of other faiths.

Churches' social engagement takes many different forms, however. Church of England churches are involved in more than 33,000 social action projects, including night shelters, community cafes, lunch clubs and youth work.[5] Based on responses from more than 1,000 Anglican church leaders, the survey found that 69 per cent of churches ran a lunch club for older people, 59 per cent ran a parent and toddler group, 32 per cent ran a community café, 30 per cent ran holiday or breakfast clubs for children, 8 per cent ran debt advice or budgeting services, and 19 per cent ran food banks. In addition to these organized activities, churches were also providing a substantial amount of informal support, particularly in response to the growing issues of loneliness and mental health, with 94 per cent and 83 per cent of churches respectively providing support for people experiencing these problems.[6]

---

4 Research and Statistics, 2017, *Statistics for Mission 2017*, London: Church of England Research and Statistics, www.church ofengland.org/sites/default/files/2018-11/2017StatisticsForMission. pdf (accessed 28 July 2019).

5 *Statistics for Mission 2017*.

6 Sefton, T.; Buckingham, H., 2018, *Church in Action: A National Survey*, Church Urban Fund. Available from www.cuf.org.uk/church-in-action-2017 (accessed 28 July 2019).

There seems to have been growth in partnership working among faith groups over the past ten years. The Church in Action survey shows that for Anglican churches, the proportion reporting that they work in partnership with other churches has increased from 41 per cent in 2014 to 62 per cent in 2018, while the proportion reporting that they work in partnership with other faith groups – although much smaller – has doubled during this time (from 4 per cent to 8 per cent). In a plural society, collaboration is likely to become increasingly important: it reflects what has been termed 'post-secular rapprochement', a coming together of people and groups who hold differing beliefs and philosophies, but share common goals or aspirations for their communities and for society.[7]

Research has shown that social action is interconnected with other aspects of church life: 64 per cent of the 1,000 Anglican church leaders surveyed as part of Church in Action 2017 agreed that 'community engagement has helped draw new people into the church' and 80 per cent agreed that 'community work helps church members to live out and grow in their Christian faith'.[8] Similarly, in *Christians in Practice*, a study of over 1,000 congregation members of Anglican churches in Birmingham and Lichfield Diocese, 78 per cent of respondents said that community engagement had helped them grow as a Christian, while 65 per cent said it had helped

7 Cloke, P.; Beaumont, J., 2012, 'Geographies of Postsecular Rapprochement in the City', *Progress in Human Geography*, 37, no. 1, 27–51, pp. 35–6.

8 *Church in Action: A National Survey (Executive Summary)*, London: Church Urban Fund. Available from www.saltleytrust. org.uk/publications/. See also www.cuf.org.uk/assets/documents/ Church_in_Action_Exec_Summary_Cover_2017.pdf (accessed 28 July 2019).

them understand their faith better.[9] The relationship between social action, discipleship and church growth is the subject of the GRA:CE project, an ongoing collaboration between Church Urban Fund and Theos.[10] Early findings from the research have highlighted the significance and distinctiveness of the relationships built in the context of social action.

One of the results of churches' increasing social action has been an increased exposure to and awareness of some of the structural injustices affecting communities and the ways policy decisions have an impact on people's lives and well-being.[11] Balancing a pastoral and practical response with a prophetic one is a challenging task, but perhaps the next step for some churches will be to explore how they can work with others to influence the drivers of poverty and help advance a vision for a more just, compassionate society.

Pro-active counting

So often our counting is reactive – a response to a request in a funding application, a defence against the questions of a prying archdeacon. But counting, measuring, evaluating and listening, telling and re-telling are powerful, illuminating tools in the fight against the injustices we see in this world.

---

9 Jones, I. (ed.), 2017, *Christians in Practice: Connecting Discipleship and Community Engagement* (Saltley Faith and Learning Series: 3), St Peter's Saltley Trust. Available from www.cuf.org.uk/assets/documents/CiP_final_report.pdf (accessed 28 July 2019).

10 See www.cuf.org.uk/research-policy/grace (accessed 28 July 2019).

11 Buckingham, H.; Jolley, A., 2015, 'Feeding the Debate: A Local Food Bank Explains Itself', *Voluntary Sector Review*, vol. 6, no. 3, pp. 311–23.

They are needed in the toolkit of any Christian activist because:

- Evaluating our social action means we can discover, celebrate, encourage. Thinking back to the Bible passage, if Matthew had not recorded that 5,000 men were fed that day (and many more women and children) or that twelve baskets of food were left over, we might not have fully understood the magnitude of this miracle. If he had not shared the small details, that Jesus was tired and grieving, we might not have been able to wonder at the compassion and generosity of our God. Discovering and sharing the stories of social action helps us celebrate what God is doing elsewhere. It was our hope in the Diocese of Liverpool that through reading about the diverse, achievable interactions of churches big and small across the diocese with their communities, others would be encouraged to do likewise.
- Evaluating means we can actually know if we are in the spaces of need (or not). Social action takes time; it is often thankless, exhausting. Recording what we are doing and with whom may seem like an added burden, more administration. But we are called to be stewards – of this earth, of our money, of our time. To be wise. Are we doing 'good' or do we just think we are? What is our Theory of Change (see box below)? Evaluating can help us listen attentively to both numbers and people, approaching humbly, working *with* rather than *on* or *for*. It can help us know where to be and who to be with – this might be in the spaces where we can be most 'effective' (where we can impact the most people, see the most 'fruitful' harvest) but it also might be in the unglamorous, forgotten spaces.
- Evaluating shows us where we can do it together. Are our churches all doing the same action? Have we collectively

forgotten some of the least, the lost, the unloved? How can we collaborate?

- Evaluating magnifies voices that need to be heard. Tirelessly God's Church chips away at systems of injustice, often under the radar. These small actions matter. Individuals matter. Quiet actions are seen by the One to whom it matters the most. But there are times to magnify, call out, stand up and throw tables over. We may need to enter the 'game' of counting, measuring, shouting, to get our cries of justice heard.

Theory of Change (Jessamin Birdsall Saunders)

What is a Theory of Change?

- A dynamic model of the processes of change that a programme aims to bring about
- Logically links the needs and assets within a particular context to the planned activities, intermediary outcomes, and long-term outcomes of a programme
- Makes explicit the assumptions of how and why change happens
- Presented visually

Why develop a Theory of Change?

- To provide a clear framework for understanding what a programme is doing and why
- To scope core outcomes to feed into an evaluation strategy
- To provide accountability for the programme

How to develop a Theory of Change?

- Convene key stakeholders – those involved in the planning, management and delivery of the programme – for a minimum of 2 hours and work through the following questions in a discussion together:
  - What are the specific needs and opportunities that your programme is best placed to address? Consider the wider set of needs/opportunities in your context, what other stakeholders are already doing, and what you have unique expertise in.
  - In 10 years' time, what specific changes would you like to see in those areas of need/opportunity? Consider changes for individual people as well as changes in the bigger structures you are engaging. These are your long-term outcomes.
  - In 5 years' time, what changes would need to be made, as intermediary steps towards the 10-year outcomes? These are your medium-term outcomes.
  - What targeted activities do you need to undertake in order to achieve those specific changes you want to see?
  - What are the key external factors (e.g. people, funding, political change) that could help or hinder you in making progress towards your outcomes?
- Consolidate your discussion notes into a one-page diagram form, which helps to clarify your thinking.

How to use a Theory of Change:

- Share with key stakeholders as a way to explain your programme and the outcomes you hope to achieve

- Revisit it with key stakeholders each year to assess programme progress, review whether your assumptions about how change happen are right, and to update as needed

For more guidance on developing your own Theory of Change, see:

https://learn.tearfund.org/~/media/files/tilz/impact_and_evaluation/2017/2017-tearfund-theory-of-change-guide-en.pdf

Tools for the toolkit

- Count what you are already doing. Notice patterns, talk about them, build this into your yearly cycle.
- Listen to (and capture) people's stories; give them space to tell them.
- Take time to reflect: who are you serving? How do you know it is what they want or need?
- Re-read the 5 marks of mission (see Rule #4 Think BIG – Start Small). What are you not doing? Why?
- Look to share what you find beyond your immediate sphere: who else might be interested? What are others doing?

Books to read

Hall, Stuart; Massey, Doreen; Rustin, Michael, 2015, *After Neo-liberalism? The Kilburn Manifesto*, London: Lawrence and Wishart.

Huxley, Justine Afra, 2019, *Generation Y, Spirituality and Social Change*, London: Jessica Kingsley.

Pickett, Kate; Wilkinson, Richard, 2010, *The Spirit Level: Why Equality is Better for Everyone*, London: Penguin.

Ritchie, Angus; Hackwood, Paul, 2014, *Just Love: Personal and Social Transformation in Christ*, Watford: Instant Apostle.

Varoufakis, Yannis, 2017, *Talking to My Daughter About the Economy: A Brief History of Capitalism*, London: Bodley Head.

Waring, Marilyn, 1988, *If Women Counted: A New Feminist Economics*, New York: HarperCollins.

Welby, Justin, 2016, *Dethroning Mammon: Making Money Serve Grace*, London: Bloomsbury Continuum.

Useful websites

Asset Based Community Development (ABCD), www2.cuf.org.uk/research-topics/abcd.

Christians Against Poverty, https://capuk.org/.

Church Urban Fund (CUF), www.cuf.org.uk/.

Five Marks of Mission, www.anglicancommunion.org/mission/marks-of-mission.aspx.

Just Finance Foundation, https://justfinancefoundation.org.uk/.

Together Liverpool, www.cuf.org.uk/together-liverpool.

Theos Thinktank, www.theosthinktank.co.uk/.

Rule #9

Remember Where You
Came From

The wrenching pain of history

History, despite its wrenching pain, cannot be unlived,
but if faced with courage, need not be lived again.[1] (Maya
Angelou)

This rule is about awareness – self-awareness, cultural awareness, religious and social awareness. It's here because there
are times in our lives when we get so carried away with being
in the present and focused on changing the future that we
forget the past that has shaped us. Both our own personal
history and the history of the places we inhabit are crucial to
making sense of how we interpret and negotiate our present.
To be activists and be ignorant of the past is like setting off
on a journey without the map (or satnav!) or putting a puzzle
together without the picture on the lid. The past has done so
much of the 'heavy lifting' in working out who we are and
what we are capable of, and we engage with present tasks
without these vital perspectives at our peril. The philosopher
George Santayana sums it up perfectly in his well-known and

---

1 1993, 'The Inauguration; Maya Angelou: "On the Pulse of
Morning"', 21 January, *New York Times*, Section A, p. 14.

often quoted phrase, 'Those who cannot remember the past are condemned to repeat it.'[2]

This chapter will explore the importance of collective and personal history by learning about and tracking a community of young people from across the world. These young people are remembering where they come from; they are interpreting their past and sharing it with those they encounter. They live in what were significant locations on the transatlantic slave-trade triangle that flourished from the sixteenth to the eighteenth centuries. The location in this case is Virginia, which exported tobacco and other raw materials to Liverpool, which in turn exported manufactured goods such as textiles, iron, beer and guns to Africa – specifically, West Africa (our particular link is with Ghana). From there, slaves were exported across the infamous 'middle passage' back to America, the West Indies and even northern parts of South America.

The historic and horrific relationship between these centres of the 'triangular trade' inspired Anglican churches in these areas to establish a different kind of relationship. This 'bond of freedom' is based on a dialogue of hope that wrestles with the complex legacy of the slave trade and the challenges of modern slavery. The 'Triangle of Hope', as it has become known, is a covenantal community involving three dioceses, dedicated to transforming the long history, ongoing effects, and continuing presence of slavery in our world through repentance, reconciliation and mission. It's a community of members who look back in order to move forward.

In this chapter, Revd Canon Malcolm Rogers, leader of the Triangle of Hope in the Diocese of Liverpool, and I will look at the importance of knowing your history, not turning aside

---

2 Santayana, George, 1905, *The Life of Reason, Vol. 1: Reason in Common Sense*, ch. 12, London: Constable.

from the difficult or uncomfortable lessons of the past but intentionally allowing the horror to speak into the present and the future. The case study will explore how the Triangle of Hope seeks to live intentionally into this, and in particular we will be looking at the Triangle's youth pilgrimages.

Jesus remembers where he comes from to form a new definition of neighbour

Just then a lawyer stood up to test Jesus. 'Teacher,' he said, 'what must I do to inherit eternal life?' He said to him, 'What is written in the law? What do you read there?' He answered, 'You shall love the Lord your God with all your heart, and with all your soul, and with all your strength, and with all your mind; and your neighbour as yourself.' And he said to him, 'You have given the right answer; do this, and you will live.'

But wanting to justify himself, he asked Jesus, 'And who is my neighbour?' Jesus replied, 'A man was going down from Jerusalem to Jericho, and fell into the hands of robbers, who stripped him, beat him, and went away, leaving him half dead. Now by chance a priest was going down that road; and when he saw him, he passed by on the other side. So likewise a Levite, when he came to the place and saw him, passed by on the other side. But a Samaritan while travelling came near him; and when he saw him, he was moved with pity. He went to him and bandaged his wounds, having poured oil and wine on them. Then he put him on his own animal, brought him to an inn, and took care of him. The next day he took out two denarii, gave them to the innkeeper, and said, "Take care of him; and when I come back, I will repay you whatever more you spend." Which of these three, do you think, was a neighbour to the man who fell into the hands of the robbers?' He said, 'The one who showed him mercy.' Jesus said to him, 'Go and do likewise.' (Luke 10.25–37)

When I was a curate in a parish in West Everton in Liverpool I was taking a baptism in one of the churches. The couple were very young – the father was wearing North Face black trousers and a jacket zipped up to the top with a peaked cap on his head, the mother was in a short white dress with white shoes and perfect make-up and hair, and the baby was bedecked in pink with an amazing bow on her head. The reading for the day was the Story of the Good Samaritan and I thought I had a reasonable sermon planned out – after all, everyone knows this story, don't they? All I had to do was come up with a few points about who your neighbour is and how it's good to be kind. I was mid-sermon when the father spoke up and said 'If that was me on the side of the road nobody would help me. I am just a scally; if they saw me, they'd definitely cross the road and think I was faking it to rob them.'

Suddenly the story came alive for all of us. We tried to disagree with the young father but actually he had a point – this young white man was exactly the sort of person we are told is dangerous, who historically, socially and culturally we must avoid. After all, he might have a knife; he might rob us and leave us on the side of the road. He really wasn't the sort of person who should be in church, let alone a person we might help – he didn't even take his hat off!

The truth is that when we examined ourselves we ended up agreeing with that young man. We agreed that we probably wouldn't help him. We would cross the road or rush on by. Until that day, when we spent an hour with him and his family, we had managed to dehumanize him. Until that conversation he was a 'type' marked out as a typical 'scally', a gang member, a hoodie, a 'rat'. But we also asked the question back at him – so, if you saw one of us on the side of the road, would you help us? He wasn't sure. He thought he might. But he couldn't promise that he would.

It is culturally acceptable for us to hate some people. This is something we have become so conditioned to that we don't even notice. It is worse than marginalizing them or treating them as 'other'. This is the opposite of love. This is hate. From this position we can pretty much do anything to anyone: we can dehumanize them, they can become our slaves, and they can be people we label and tag (hence the tagging of young white boys as 'rats'). In the case of the history shared by Jews and Samaritans, their hatred of each other made it impossible for this young Jewish lawyer to imagine a Samaritan as a person, let alone someone who could be a neighbour. He asks with an existing definition based on his religious and historical framework, but Jesus goes right back to basics (Leviticus 19) to recast the Samaritan as the good neighbour in order to push past cultural boundaries. By recasting it he is challenging the supposition that it is all right to hate.

The danger is that history, social and religious convention and cultural expectations limit us. If we have the courage to remember your history and not be confined by it, we can do much more than learn: we can shift the present and the future into a new story of hope, like a piece of jewellery that over time becomes out of shape, tarnished or broken but can be refashioned into something beautiful and new.

We remember where we come from in order to distil contemporary faith so that we remove the impurities that can build up over time. It refocuses us on our blessings and our shared stories, not those that drive us apart.

The Triangle of Hope

Knowing your history and remembering where you come from is a key component of the work that is done by young people taking part in the Triangle of Hope youth pilgrimages. The 'journey' begins from the moment of the first session of the two-year programme, certainly prior to any trips or hosting. Three groups set off together, one in each diocese, exploring their own local history as well as the history that connects us. We listen and we share stories; we use technologies to forge deep bonds and we do this intentionality with a common purpose of creating a new future together.

The 'curriculum' covers the history of the transatlantic slave trade. The three-way dialogue means that the young people lead from each country and experience. When they visit each other they explore their history and share their present. These exchanges trips only happen after serious reflection (they are not tourist trips!) with the young people, interpreting the country visited in terms of both historical perspectives and current cultural and religious experience. The pilgrim is expected to be able to interact with complex narratives and sometimes paradoxical experiences.

An example of this is found in Liverpool, where the slave trade is often discreetly hidden or goes unnoticed to modern eyes. Youth pilgrims spend a lot of time 'revisiting' their home city, its famous streets (named after slave owners and traders, e.g. Rodney Street and Penny Lane), and its wonderful architecture (paid for by wealthy slave merchants). There is always horror and silence and disbelief when they visit a white-stoned doorway, just off Castle Street behind the Parish Church and near the town hall. This is the entrance to Martins Bank. The bank is now closed but in the eighteenth and nineteenth centuries it played a key role in the financial affairs of the slave trade. So important were these 'human cargoes' in fact that the triangular trade is depicted in its very design. If you asked most Liverpudlians today if there was a building in a very prominent place in the city that around its entrance has proudly depicted African children in chains and holding money bags, they would say no and would be rightly appalled at the thought of it. They would be unlikely to be able to tell you where it was – and yet it's right there in the city centre and thousands of people walk past it every day. Youth pilgrims spend a lot of time in the internationally renowned Slavery Museum and speak to people for whom racism and the impact of hatred continue to disempower and dehumanize.

John Newton wrote his remarkable song 'Amazing Grace' about how his conversion to following Christ was like a sweet song that spoke truth into his heart and lifted the scales from his eyes. When he writes 'I was blind but now I see' he was looking out at the world with the new eyes of Christ and saw that the dehumanizing of others in slavery was unacceptable. He became an antislavery activist and helped to change the course of history.

Our unacceptable history is often (and rightly) a burden of shame. It has always been shameful but we allow its sinfulness to become our sin when we convince ourselves that it is simply historical fact and not a contemporary evil. In Richmond, Virginia, on the banks of James River, there is a route that the enslaved Africans were forced to take after disembarking from the ships in the middle of the night. Slaves were moved at night in order to spare white middle-class people the shame of having to see them being transported. This is a profoundly disturbing place for those who know their history, and the pilgrims make the same journey in silence, and in the middle of the day, out of respect. On one occasion the group was nearing a place where an interstate highway crosses the river.

They came across two white men who were spending the afternoon fishing. Puzzled by the presence of a large group of young people in a place now seldom visited, they asked what the group was doing. Young people began to share the history of the route and the importance of the site. Hearing them speak about their learning was in itself moving but something then happened that would burn deep into all our learning. An African American delivery man pulled his truck over. He knew why the group was there, and he was so thankful that his-story, our-story, was being remembered. 'Thank you for remembering,' he said. The juxtaposition of the responses to the presence of these pilgrims was overwhelming – ignorance and gratitude, thankfulness and remembering.

In rural Ghana, the pilgrims are encouraged to record their learning using technology such as photos on their mobile phones. These aren't selfies or holiday snaps, they are reminders to help them hold on to what they see and what they felt. At the end of each day the group uses these to reflect more formally on the impact of the day. However, part of the learning is the very evident environmental damage done by companies in Ghana who extract minerals for the production of the very technology in their hands – this leads to a real inner wrestling as the pilgrims work out how they can live with integrity 'back home'. We have seen pilgrims upgrading their phones much less regularly, recycling where possible and also challenging the mobile phone companies directly, in particular how they deal with the water-polluting waste created by the extraction processes. There is another paradox they encounter. Many of the larger companies 'investing' in Africa are contributing to infrastructure, new roads, hospitals and even airports. This clearly is motivated by the opportunity to increase profit or secure a base for raw materials needed 'back home'. It is a complex and at times deeply disturbing narrative, of deals done that seem to echo the internal horrors and dehumanization of fellow Africans that partly enabled the slave trade. Decisions are made by the powerful at the expense of the poorest. This tension is present in most explorations and processes of learning. Discerning responses and moving through these tensions is crucial to deep learning.

It is this deeper level of questioning that is required for Christian activists as they prepare to journey into history and remember the past. There's a poem by Martha Postlethwaite that is used as a pilgrimage gets underway. It's called 'Clearing'.[3]

> Do not try to save
> the whole world
> or do anything grandiose.
> Instead, create
> a clearing
> in the dense forest
> of your life
> and wait there
> patiently,
> until the song
> that is yours alone to sing
> falls into your open cupped hands
> and you recognize and greet it.
> Only then will you know
> how to give yourself
> to this world so worthy of rescue.

Whether we are travelling abroad or seeking interior transformation at home, it's vital that we begin by taking stock of who and where and what we are. It isn't clear if Martha

3 Postlethwaite, M., 2019, *Addiction and Recovery: A Spiritual Pilgrimage*, Minneapolis, MN: Fortress Press.

writes from a Christian perspective, but 'Clearing' is reminiscent of R. S. Thomas's seminal poem 'Kneeling', in which he concludes 'The meaning is in the waiting'.[4] This form of 'centring' or focusing requires us to be honest and open. Our work as Christian activists requires every ability, defence and resilience, for the world we encounter day by day has pretty much turned its back on God and the vision for a kingdom built on justice, peace and joy (Romans 14). Even so, being prepared for the journey God has called us to take requires a vulnerability that in itself can so often be squeezed out by activism. We need to create and keep creating a clearing. We need to clear the debris. And at times, even when we are motivated to activity, we need to wait – wait and recall and reflect. For it is in that place that we shall discern our next steps and direction, faced with so many pathways we could travel down to fight injustice; it is there we receive what we need. The image Martha paints of our unique song, our purpose falling into open cupped hands, is reminiscent of the way we take communion, God making himself known to us in Christ as bread is broken. Here in the dense, busy places of our lives, when we clear our space for waiting, as we open up our hands and our hearts, God comes to us. He promises to do so, as Isaiah reminds us so wonderfully:

> But they that wait upon the LORD shall renew their strength; they shall mount up with wings as eagles; they shall run, and not be weary; and they shall walk, and not faint. (Isaiah 40.31 KJV)

So put down and leave behind those things that are not of God. It's hard not to fall into the trap of becoming 'the white and male saviour' when travelling in and out of Africa.

---

4 Thomas, R. S., 1995, 'Kneeling', in *Collected Poems 1945–1990*, London: Phoenix, p. 199.

Colonial history still distorts God's vision for Africa and for me. A key component of the work of the Triangle of Hope is restoring that vision in which all are equal, all are beloved children of God. So when we check into hotels in Ghana and the white members of the group are given significantly better rooms than our African travelling companions, it is important for us to have the conversation with the hotel manager. 'Why is this happening?' Similarly, before we even get on the plane, it's important to ask the question, 'Why am I doing this?'

'Sankofa' comes from the Akan language of Twi and is a word we often use in the Triangle of Hope. Literally, it means 'Go back and get it.' It's represented in the Asante Adinkra symbols (where the Triangle of Hope logo comes from by kind permission of the Asante King) as a bird journeying forward but with its head backwards.

It's vitally important that anyone involved in Christian activism is self-aware – not in a self-obsessed or self-destructive way, but remembering Jesus' summary of the commandments in Matthew 22. But looking back is part of moving forward, knowing that God who is 'the same, yesterday, today and for ever' (Hebrews 13.8) can bring light out of darkness and that because the 'God who calls you is faithful' (1 Thessalonians 5.24) he can use each of us to make a real difference in the world today.

We look back in different ways. Here in Liverpool we reflect on our great city, built from the profits of the slave trade. We think about how even our diocese profited. We consider how our lives today continue to profit from exploitation. This looking back forces us to look around and examine again the landscape of injustice in our great city, challenging us to listen and respond to what God is saying about today's injustice to God's people today.

In our 'cleared space' we opened our hands waiting upon God for the song God wants us to sing. Now, it's as if these same open hands, in similar eucharistic imagery, are called to receive, and serve today's victims of injustice, all children of God. Christian activism must have as its foundation the centrality of Christ if it is to be truly authentic.

Tools for the toolkit

- Know your history.
- Revisit regularly who you are in the light of history – unconscious bias, power.
- Be prepared to be open to change (embark on your pilgrimages whether at home or abroad intentionally – they will change you if you let them!).
- Fight the urge to be benevolent (you are not the saviour of the world – Jesus is!).
- Learning from history is exhausting, so look after yourself – take notes and rest.
- Christian activism will exhaust and frustrate you, and might not make you popular. Cherish those who sustain you.
- Be alert to those times when you are compelled by your understanding and experience to speak out against injustice (often when you least expect it) and challenge the narrative. Even so, do so with humility.
- Once you see 'it' you can't unsee it. Be prepared for what that means.
- Stay focused on Jesus.

Books to read

Akala, 2019, *Natives: Race and Class in the Ruins of Empire*, London: Two Roads.

Beckford, Robert, 2004, *God and the Gangs*, London: Darton, Longman and Todd.

Brueggemann, Walter, 2001, *Hope for the World: Mission in a Global Context*, Louisville, KY: Westminster John Knox Press.

Eddo-Lodge, Reni, 2018, *Why I'm No Longer Talking to White People About Race*, London: Bloomsbury.

Pye, Ken, 2019, *Two Triangles: Liverpool, Slavery and the Church*, Diocese of Liverpool and USPG.

Shukla, Nikesh, 2017, *The Good Immigrant*, London: Unbound.

Stormzy, 2018, *Rise Up: The #Merky Story So Far*, London: #Merky Books.

Threlfall-Holmes, Miranda, 2012, *The Essential History of Christianity*, London: SPCK.

Viola, Frank; Demuth, Mary, 2015, *The Day I Met Jesus: The Revealing Diaries of Five Women from the Gospels*, Grand Rapids, MI: Baker Books.

Useful websites

The Clewer Initiative, www.theclewerinitiative.org/.
USPG, www.uspg.org.uk/.
Stop the Traffik, www.stopthetraffik.org/.
Modern Slavery Lessons, www.modernslaveryeducation.com/.

Rule #10

Take Risks

Take a deep breath

There are going to be times in your life when things get very difficult – times when being a Christian activist is like being stuck in a quagmire and you're wading through mud. You might find that occasionally you need to watch your back or do something about an injustice that is staring you in the face. If you are not a natural risk-taker, the idea of stepping out may feel overwhelming. If you are a natural risk-taker, there will be times when you need to take a deep breath and weigh up the pros and cons and perhaps hold back. But what is important is that you don't try and go it alone. You need the backup of good people who share your concerns and you need to have taken the risk to God and prayerfully considered the consequences. There will be consequences and some of those may be hard to handle. The ride might be bumpy but it will be an adventure.

This is my story, a story of success and failure – but it is mainly about taking risks. It is a story of my time as vicar at St Luke the Evangelist, Walton – a parish church that is situated next to Everton Football Club. It is a story of how the PCC decided to take the risk of praying for, and inviting, ten new families to come and change the way worship and community life would be lived out. It will also tell you about how this didn't exactly go to plan and explain how the project created sadness and hurt for some. This chapter is about how taking risks, stepping out and trying new things can provoke change. The chapter will give you some ideas about how to navigate new territories and keep records of your adventures.

Sheep, wolves, serpents and doves

> I am sending you out like sheep with wolves all around you. Be wise like snakes and gentle like doves. (Matthew 10.16 NLV)

Jesus is speaking to his friends – the people who have already taken massive risks to be his disciples. They have given up their families, homes and livelihood in order to follow him – and it has been an amazing adventure. They have learnt to trust Jesus; they have seen miraculous healings, been part of a new narrative around the coming kingdom, seen God at work in their community and witnessed Jesus' challenge to the authorities and religious leaders. They have also heard Jesus speaking to them, and the massed crowds, in ways that inspired them to think of life way beyond their own experience. Just before this cautious private conversation, Jesus spoke boldly in what we refer to as 'the sermon on the mount' (Matthew 6—8). The sermon outlines Jesus' manifesto and priorities, and he also teaches about prayer and spiritual purpose.

Anyway, back to the passage we are looking at … Having called them, inspired them and spent time teaching them, Jesus is now warning his new friends. He is warning them that the adventure they are on will not always be easy. Indeed, the outcome of the work he is setting before them will certainly be very hard. It is difficult to imagine what Jesus is speaking about because most of us will not have suffered persecution, the majority of us will have found faith easy and few of us will have been through what the disciples eventually end up experiencing. But what Jesus was calling them to was the biggest risk of all – the life-changing risk of stepping out of the Jewish tradition and the occupied forces' legal framework. They were moving into uncharted territory and letting go of all the social constructs around them. As such, this group of people were a dangerous bunch and things were going to get very hard indeed. The harsh reality of their life choices must have become stark. The words of Jesus here are not comforting but they are realistic. He knew the risks and he was urging them to face these and prepare for the road ahead. They may not have known exactly what he was saying but the reality was that they were heading for Jerusalem on a journey that would lead to the death of their leader and the disintegration of their group.

So what is his advice? How does he counsel his friends?

Well, he tells them to be as wise as serpents and gentle as doves. I wonder if they looked at Jesus the way I looked at Jane Corbett (you've met Jane in Chapter 5) when she said this to me after a particularly intense conversation with a political leader who was determined to ignore the voices of the community? I was close to behaving rashly but Jane urged me to be patient – patient but not naive. She urged me to go away and do more work on my plan. And eventually (it took ages) I found a way to enter into a dialogue with this person that had more impact.

Often as Christians we are thought of as gentle doves but not always that wise. Indeed, the idea of being wise serpents might seem a bit scheming and even unchristian. But right from the heart of Jesus' teaching, he is telling us we need to wise up and do the background checks, make sure we know what we are doing, plan, watch our backs, use our senses. Christians are not pushovers – we are empowered, holy and set aside to seek God's will. This demands us to have our heads screwed on but not screw people over.

Being wise means planning; risk-taking needs a lot of weighing up. It's no good risking if you don't know what you might lose or indeed what you might gain. So be a careful risk-taker. Also, what to you is a risk well weighed may be a very frightening life change for someone else. There is no need for your risk to run roughshod over all and sundry – though the wisdom bit might tell you that not everyone is going to be happy with the risk, you can avoid rubbing people's noses in it. Finding wise and gentle ways to take risk is my advice (for what it's worth).

The risk of failure

Having served my curacy in West Everton in the north end of the city of Liverpool, I had felt a strong calling to stay in this part of the diocese. The church I felt called to had not had a vicar for a couple of years – the last vicar had reluctantly retired after a long incumbency, which had left the small congregation feeling isolated and unsupported by the diocese and suspicious of their neighbouring churches. It was a church that was not growing in numbers and, while it had a lot of assets (two big halls and a meeting room, wonderful garden and well-looked-after church), it was not sharing these with the community they could be serving. The isolation the church congregation felt had created a disconnection from the people in the community that surrounded them. The hall lay empty most of the week, it was full of church treasures and old equipment used in the past but not very useful for the future. The garden was beautiful but very rarely visited by local people. The church was open for a couple of hours on Sunday and Thursday evening and on match days but otherwise was a fortress covered in barbed wire. A small and dedicated team had preserved the integrity of the legacy of the previous incumbent and were very protective. They were very sad that he had left. Looking back now I am not sure they were very happy that I arrived. But at first I didn't notice because I felt a strong calling to this parish and despite the fact that there was no vicarage and there were a lot of challenges to be faced, I really wanted to be there. This was the first risk: the risk of falling in love with a ministry, a place and a group of people. If you take that risk then you have to be willing to see it through even when things go wrong. As so often with love, there are times when it's not possible to fight it, and this was one of those times.

The parish is an area of urban deprivation. Most of the families in the area are on very low incomes. The parish has few central places where the community can gather, and as a result there is little in the way of a sense of community space. The area is a play desert with limited facilities for children and, with the exception of places to gamble, and a pub, and Everton football ground, no place for adult leisure activities. The church itself is attached to the football ground, meaning that the area is highly congested on match days, the population growing from 7,000 to 45,000 for just a few hours.

The parish has no green space and housing is predominantly small terraces that open directly on to the street, with no back gardens and possibly only a small yard. Some 22 per cent of families live in social housing – and many more live in private tenancies without the support and regulations of a housing association. The community is therefore chaotic and transient and becoming more so with government welfare reform and the introduction of the bedroom tax and universal credit.

Around 47 per cent of children are living in poverty, 43 per cent of households have no qualifications, 57 per cent of households are lone parents and only 13 per cent are aged 65 or older. This means we have a much higher proportion of children and young people in the area than the national average, and most of these are being brought up in single-parent homes, with a history of long-term unemployment, and as such many live in poverty.[1]

This urban ministry is where my heart is – as well as thinking I could make a real difference, I also felt that there was a real possibility that the place and people would change me. I hoped it would be a chance for me to be part of something exciting, fresh, challenging and risky. So I was installed as priest in charge at St Luke's on 13 March 2012 (I was licensed as Area Dean six months later and in 2014 I was licensed as Vicar).

One of the best things about the parish ministry was match-day 'teas for fans'. The close proximity of the church to the football club home ground meant that match days were festival days. The church served tea and sandwiches and cake and opened the garden up for fans to pray and rest in. Many of these fans had relatives whose ashes were buried in the garden, so this ministry was significant. The church congregation came alive on match days; there was a buzz and real sense of camaraderie and possibility. But it was hard work and the congregation was aging. We needed 25–40 people volunteering to pull off providing sandwiches and cake,

---

1 For a full and accurate picture of the Index of Multiple Deprivation, please use the Church Urban Fund Poverty Map (www2.cuf.org.uk/poverty-england/poverty-map) .

making tea for thousands of fans, selling programmes and being hospitable. The constant filling of urns, washing of tea cups, moving of furniture and cleaning of toilets was taking its toll on everyone. There wasn't a lot of spare time or energy for any other significant ministry.

I had decided that for the first six months I wouldn't make any changes. Instead I intended to wait and observe what was working and what was hurting. It was very difficult. Everything seemed to hurt: my just being there was painful, my not being the previous incumbent was like a knife twisting and my asking them to join in change was just too much. By the end of the first football season I wasn't sure if I would be able to help revive the church, make it financially independent or help it connect with the community again. I was exhausted but I didn't understand that the church congregation were exhausted and demoralized too. They had been holding this together for years and I had only been there for a few months. I didn't understand that they needed me to help them do less, not ask them to do more.

When I applied for the role, the 'parish profile' (this is like an advert for the job – it contains information about the parish and explains the church's vision) made it clear that they wanted to open up the vast parish halls for community use and that they wanted to be a family church – attracting young people and children from the local schools. They wanted change and I was there to lead them through this change. What was clear was that this change would be completely at my risk. There would be no funds available from the parish church council (PCC) and they would help out on new initiatives only on their terms.

So here is the second risk: the risk of failure. Whatever risk you take there will be a good chance it won't work out. Therefore preparing yourself for the possibility of failure is very important. I had already fallen in love with the church, the place and the people, but now I was risking failure. I felt quite alone – just a few people supporting the change and I had no resources to make change happen. If you can't bear that risk then it is possibly not worth persisting. I decided it was worth the risk, and anyway, what did I have to lose now there was so much stacked against me? So I cracked on.

During the interregnum the experienced reader and church-warden (a married couple who lived about 8 miles away) had piloted Messy Church with the support of a Christian local youth organization called Ykids.[2] This was very successful and clearly inspired the couple's interest in developing this work. So together we formed a partnership that would eventually lead to a series of Messy Church events and a weekly 'super club' for under-10s that was like Sunday school on a Thursday. By Christmas we had a lot of children coming and it was obvious that we needed more helpers and more resources. We needed to clear the halls to make them safe and create space for children to play and adults to rest. The hall clearance took a week and five skips and a lot of heartache. Myself and a few of the less exhausted church members helped, but mainly it was volunteers from the football club charity that made the hall transformation possible.

The halls could then be opened up to other groups: a martial arts group began renting one hall three times a week, AA and NA took the meeting room twice a week, a scout group returned, a lunch club and a craft group ('crafter-noons') sprang up and the existing 'pram club' and Mothers Union continued. I applied for some funding and we started a few extra projects: a community choir, a young people's drama group and a dance club. We linked with a local secondary school and the Anne Frank Trust; more external

2 www.ykids.co.uk/.

funding led to an exhibition being staged in the church for a week and over 1,000 young people visited to learn about the Holocaust. This initiative led to the development of a programme of events the following year that included a concert and a play being staged, and 24 hours of prayer attended by local young people. The link with our local community primary school developed and children would often come into church for festivals and celebrations.

The biggest change came when we were approached by a pre-school who wanted a place to open up a morning session. They would be able to pay for upgrading facilities and then offer significant rent for the space. However, they needed a five-year agreement and sole use of one hall every morning. It was possible and reluctantly the PCC agreed. This one decision would mean that the church was financially viable for the next five years.

This was a time of excitement and change. It was also a time of anxiety and stress for the existing church community. They felt they had not always been included in all aspects of the change; it was happening very fast and they didn't have full emotional investment in the new groups. Despite being very clear that I wasn't going to change anything about the traditional Eucharist on Sunday morning or make any changes to the main worship pattern or the main church space, they still felt anxious. There were strangers occupying the hall space that they had had sole use of for decades. For them it was still a church hall and not a community hall. The implications of the shift were dawning on them and it was met with some resistance. Most of the clashes might have been prevented if I had planned a bit more carefully, asked a few more questions of the church community about when they needed access and shared some of the relationship connections more effectively. My calculation was that they were unable (or unwilling) to invest money or time, so if what they asked for was to happen I had to seek this from outside the tired beleaguered group who were constantly cross with me. I ended up driving change through a lot harder than I had wished to and I recognize that this was unacceptable to some of the long-standing members of the congregation.

Then two things changed: first, I received significant funding that paid for two community family workers to take up some of the work; second, we got a curate who had a vision for starting a new family congregation from scratch. For me this was to be the end of a very lonely part of my ministry. The close connections with community groups and new families set off at a new and exciting pace. We became more strategic. We set targets and measured success (and failure).

Working with Ykids, the local schools and the new team, we began what we called the Luke 18.16 Project. Its name is based on the Gospel verse:

> But Jesus called for them and said, 'Let the little children come to me, and do not stop them; for it is to such as these that the kingdom of God belongs.'

This project aimed to bring together the vision the PCC had started with, to bring children into the church and extend the use of the halls (even though they had become disconnected from it) and start a new phase of the development of the work that had flourished in the previous two years.

Our vision was that the Luke 18.16 project would bring:

- Community cohesion – the church would become an anchor in the chaotic lives of many children and families.
- Well-being – enabling young people to feel valued, loved and supported, with a place to be and to belong.

- Witness – we would be the hands and feet of Jesus in our community, offering love, support, welcome, acceptance and hope to young people who often feel rejected and unwanted.
- Emotional resilience – help to build young people's abilities to deal with life, make better choices and break cycles of hopelessness, worklessness, low attainment and low aspirations.
- Increase positive mental health – provide opportunities for the community to engage in the five ways of well-being, which are: Get connected, Talk, Give, Exercise and Enable people to see the 'wow factor'.
- All of these can be measured by our impact measurement tool and individual case studies.

In the two years (2015–17) that the project ran it had an incredible impact. A new family and children's hub had been established, with a weekly after-school club, weekly pram club, monthly SEN support group, monthly boys' group, and a weekly craft group and choir for parents as well, as half-term and summer activities and trips. Our summer street play saw three different families involved in engaging with their community, providing play activities and friendship to their neighbours. Additionally, we had three families now responsible for running the weekly pram club with supervision from our salaried family workers. We managed to recruit 18 volunteers who between them clocked up over 800 hours of volunteering over the two years. Over the course of the two years we had the opportunity to work with over 100 registered children of around 65 families; 40 of these families were on a regular (weekly or fortnightly) basis.

The numbers speak for themselves, but qualitative changes in people's lives were just as informative and wonderful to witness.

Below is a selection of quotes from people we worked with:

'Can we do this every week? Sit around the table to eat and talk about God?' – 11-year-old boy.
'I am so glad kids club was on today, my girl has been crying about going to secondary school' – Mum.
'I never left the house before I came here, except to go to school' – Mum (Crafternoons).
'I'm loving this, have you a toddler group I can help in too?' – New Mum (Volunteer).
'I'm sorry for what I said last week about X, when I got home I thought "that was really mean" so I'm sorry. I take it back' – Mum reflecting on her own response to offering hospitality to someone she struggled with.
'This is the first church I have felt welcomed in. I've wanted to come back for a while and it was hard to leave the house but I knew once I got here I'd be okay' – Mum returning to church after time away dealing with anxiety and depression.

It was going so well, we had exceeded all our targets and were working effectively as a staff team. The family café church congregation was flourishing, every week new people came to worship on Sunday or Thursday and new initiatives began to emerge from the community. It was a very exciting place to be; we had moved from transactors (giving/taking) to participants (sharing).

Then it all changed – I got a new job.

I had not planned to move on after just four years but the new role was an opportunity I felt I couldn't turn down. Anyway, there were three experienced, wonderful women working on the project and surely the PCC must have bought into the project, having seen the wonderful changes in the community and new people coming to church and meeting Jesus there?

What I had underestimated was the level of discontent that had been simmering in the background. Resentment at my making so many changes, which was only compounded when I announced my resignation and the hurt deepened. The traditional congregation and the long-standing members of the church had become so disconnected from this new work that they felt they wanted it to end – feeling that it was my work and not theirs, the PCC withdrew their backing. Despite putting in supervision from a neighbouring parish, the family workers and curate were more vulnerable and less supported than anyone could have imagined. Their position became untenable and they had all left within six months of my departure, and money raised for their wages and projects was returned to funders. The mainstay of the project ended.

Seeing the work end like this was heartbreaking. The rejection of the work, not just my work but the work of so many in the community and some in the church, was painful. I felt so sure that the change was right, I was convinced that it would bring life and new vision to a community that really needed hope; but then seeing it packed up, equipment returned and the money sent back to funders – well, that was devastating. Even though I wasn't their vicar anymore and I had no pastoral oversight, I wept and wept for them. I cried for the personal rejection of the vision and the deep rejection of the work – not just my work but the work of so many. I also felt the sadness of the group of people who had obviously been feeling rejected and angry for such a long time, the deep anger they must have felt to think it necessary to wipe out the hard work of others and the good that had been done. I thought it was the end. I thought that the families whose lives we had seen changed by their hearing of the gospel of Jesus would be lost. I had to accept that it was over. I wasn't there anymore.

Obviously, this is just one side of the story – it's my story of risk and success and failure and this is the way I am telling it here. But this is the honesty I wanted to share with you. We hear so many stories of marvellous ministries but the reality is that it is often a hard slog littered with rejection and rumpled risk. The question is, is it worth it?

Well, for a long time I couldn't bear to think about it. I was despised by the majority of my former PCC, people I thought were friends rejected me, I was even unfriended on Facebook, shouted at when I visited, and spoken about cruelly behind my back. But not by everyone – just a few kept in touch (mostly the new families). A new vicar arrived and these new families stuck with him; they began to flourish under his care, as did the older members of the congregation. Love has crept back in and changes continue to emerge. Under Frank's gentle but focused leadership they have moved on to another stage in the church's life.

I have told you this story, a very personal story, and as you read it you could probably think of loads of things you would have done differently. I wonder if you think that I was unwise to let myself become so invested? Or was I too hard – if I had been gentler (as a dove), would I have brought people along with me more effectively? Perhaps I was wise to crack on because I saw the injustice of the people unable to get into church and hear the good news, and gentle in the way I persisted even in the face of resistance – offering gentle care to the people who had missed out on the glory of church life for so long. Perhaps you would have taken more risks – or fewer! You might have found ways to keep people alongside and inside the project. Maybe you would have gone slower or perhaps just not cared at all about what went before but steamrollered over it all. Indeed, I am sure every one of us would have done it differently. I can look back and think of loads of things I would have done differently (though I think in the end it would have turned out pretty much the same way).

All of this is speculation and my 'what-ifs?' are not the main reason for telling you this story. Why I wanted you to read this, why 'Take Risks' is one of my rules, is because risk-taking is a basic foundation of our faith. The reason Jesus spoke to his disciples about wisdom and gentleness was because he knew they were embarking on high-risk activities. Making a difference, seeing more justice in the world – this is a risky business. If you are really ready for taking risks for Jesus and really committed to social action and making a difference, it is very likely that something like this will happen to you (if it hasn't already happened). It is very unlikely that you will take risks that everyone is happy about. It's very likely that you will make mistakes and mess something up. But when you take risks, things change. Perhaps you'll be fortunate and take risks that everyone applauds you for and you become famous for your success and everyone loves you – in which case I take my hat off to you.

I didn't set out to be mean or thoughtless. I am not a lone, maverick, alpha leader in need of personal glory. I prayed a lot about all of this, I spoke to trusted colleagues about change management and genuinely tried to embed change and develop co-owned practice. Much of what happened excited a lot of people, lives were changed and people came to know Christ for the first time and in a new way. I came to know Christ in a new way. My continued prayers are for the gentle breath of wisdom to flow through all of us who were changed by what happened, and that God's love and mercy will win out.

Tools for the toolkit

- Check yourself: are you hungry? Tired? Lonely? If you are then sort that out first.
- Prayer – this goes without saying, but as we know, it has to be said because just like the first thing, sometimes when we are under pressure we forget the basics.
- Never do anything rash when you are angry – my grandfather told me once after a particularly big row with my grandmother that he had learnt to 'never put his head in the oven when it was hot'. He would let anger cool down before embarking on any further action. This advice is good advice.
- Who are your allies and are they going to stick with you? Find out who is still up for staying with the risk you have started taking. If you are completely on your own, you might need to have a rethink. Start with people already involved before you seek new allies and advice.
- Go back to the impact and what you have achieved. Reassess and examine this intensively – use your allies to help you do this.
- Look at the original aims and objectives – you might need to check that the path you're on is still aligned to these; use your allies to help you do this.
- Re-assess and make changes if you really need to but don't do this until you have done everything else above (You might lose your original allies here. Ask whether it is worth it.)

> • If all else fails – walk away. Pack everything up as neatly as possible, make a good record of the experience and try to leave kindly. If following this route I would recommend doing the painful task of grieving as quickly as possible. Don't put it off. Live with the hurt, experience every level and depth of it and learn as much as you can from the experience of risk you have undertaken.

Books to read

Ahern, Geoffrey, 1987, *Inner City God: The Nature of Belief in the Inner City*, London: Hodder & Stoughton.

Beasley-Murray, Paul, 1992, *Radical Believers: The Baptist Way of Being the Church*, Wallingford: Baptist Union of Great Britain.

Chester, Tim, 2012, *Unreached: Growing Churches in Working-class and Deprived Areas*, Nottingham: IVP.

Claiborne, Shane, 2006, *The Irresistible Revolution: Living as an Ordinary Radical*, Grand Rapids, MI: Zondervan.

Davey, Andrew, 2010, *Crossover City: Resources for Urban Mission and Transformation*, London: Mowbray.

Eastman, Michael; Latham, Steve, 2004, *Urban Church: A Practitioner's Resource Book*, London: SPCK.

Lane, Chris, 2017, *Ordinary Miracles: Mess, Meals and Meeting Jesus in Unexpected Places*, Watford: Instant Apostle.

Martin, Jim, 2012, *The Just Church: Becoming a Risk-taking, Justice-seeking, Disciple-making Congregation*, Carol Stream, IL: Tyndale House Publishers.

McGarvey, Darren, 2018, *Poverty Safari: Understanding the Anger of Britain's Underclass*, London: Picador.

Witherington, Ben, 2001, *The Gospel of Mark: A Socio-rhetorical Commentary*, Grand Rapids, MI: Eerdmans.

Useful websites

Urban Matthew, www.urbanmatthew.co.uk.
Urban Theology Unit, http://utusheffield.org.uk/.
Sojourners USA, https://sojo.net/.
Red Letter Christians, https://redletterchristians.org.uk/.

Rule #11

Travel Light

HOW TO BE A POET
(to remind myself)
Make a place to sit down.
Sit down. Be quiet.
You must depend upon
affection, reading, knowledge,
skill – more of each
than you have – inspiration,
work, growing older, patience,
for patience joins time
to eternity. Any readers
who like your poems,
doubt their judgment.
Breathe with unconditional breath
the unconditioned air.
Shun electric wire.
Communicate slowly. Live
a three-dimensioned life;
stay away from screens.
Stay away from anything
that obscures the place it is in.
There are no unsacred places;
there are only sacred places
and desecrated places.

Accept what comes from silence.
Make the best you can of it.
Of the little words that come
out of the silence, like prayers
prayed back to the one who prays,
make a poem that does not disturb
the silence from which it came.[1]

Accept what comes from silence

Wendell Berry's graceful counsel on how to be a poet is also great advice for gentle activists (to remind ourselves). This rule is particularly useful for those of us who need to balance out our busyness with some silence and who need to remember that this is a work of peace, not simply a hive of activity. The good news we announce, the kingdom we proclaim, is that of love and peace and hope. If it comes out of our mouths or our actions as a shout of triumph or a heavy-footed stamp of ignorance, then we will not be heard.

We are called to be different, to be a living sacrifice of God's love for the world. One of the ways that makes us different is that we share the load of our activism with each other and should not become overburdened. We are not the saviours of the world; Jesus has that covered. What we are called to do is to play a part in the time we have been allocated and do this as well as we can to the glory of God. We are not called to trample all over other people in order to achieve our aims or to forget the bigger picture of God's salvation. Only we can do what God has called us to and this should be offered as freely and as gently as possible.

---

1 Berry, Wendell, 2012, 'How to be a Poet', *New Collected Poems*, Berkeley, CA: Counterpoint Press.

One of the dangers as activists is that we get so caught up in the doing that we forget about being. When we hear God's call to 'be still' (Psalm 46.10), this is not a call to inactivity but to the purposeful demand to exist in the presence of God. None of this activism will make any lasting impact if it is not connected through the power of the Holy Spirit. We live together as the people of God connected as Christ's body in the knowledge of God's eternal love. The Wisdom of God knows what our soul longs for and she should not be disregarded. Wisdom calls with her still, soft voice; ignoring this whisper can lead to a separation that disrupts and dislocates.

This chapter is about how we might be gentle activists – how we listen to the Holy Spirit, how we pray, how we live unburdened lives. The Bible reflection that follows was written by me and the case study about travelling light has been written by Fr Richard Peers. Here he reflects on his personal spiritual practice, his work in schools and churches and how we might learn the gentle art of travelling light from Augustine, the practice of mindfulness and a personal rule of life.

'Travel light. Comb and toothbrush and no extra luggage'[2]

After this the Lord appointed seventy others and sent them on ahead of him in pairs to every town and place where he himself intended to go. He said to them, 'The harvest is plentiful, but the labourers are few; therefore ask the Lord of the harvest to send out labourers into his harvest. Go on your way. See, I am sending you out like lambs into the midst of wolves. Carry no purse, no bag, no sandals;

---

2 Luke 10.4a (MSG).

and greet no one on the road. Whatever house you enter, first say, "Peace to this house!" And if anyone is there who shares in peace, your peace will rest on that person; but if not, it will return to you. Remain in the same house, eating and drinking whatever they provide, for the labourer deserves to be paid. Do not move about from house to house. Whenever you enter a town and its people welcome you, eat what is set before you; cure the sick who are there, and say to them, "The kingdom of God has come near to you." But whenever you enter a town and they do not welcome you, go out into its streets and say, "Even the dust of your town that clings to our feet, we wipe off in protest against you. Yet know this: the kingdom of God has come near."' (Luke 10.1–11)

This biblical account of the sending out of the 70 (plus the 2 who had already been sent) is a story of action. These people are being sent, just as John the Baptist had been previously, to prepare Jesus' way. But this time they are going in pairs; there are to be no maverick heroics, they are called to gently and carefully bring peace to the places they visit. Then Jesus will follow.

The action of being sent comes with some practical guidance from Jesus, who reminds them that they are to remain gentle lambs even among the wolves. Their worldly wisdom should not override their gentle calling[3] and they also need to remember whose reputation they are representing: they go as Jesus' messengers. And then we get an insight into Jesus' peripatetic practice: travel light; go gently, or as the Message translation of verses 4–6 has it:

---

3 Remember Rule #10 Take Risks, and Matthew 10.16, wise as serpents and gentle as doves.

Travel light. Comb and toothbrush and no extra luggage.
Don't loiter and make small talk with everyone you meet
along the way.
When you enter a home, greet the family, 'Peace'.

Jesus, by his own example, wants his 'workers for the harvest'[4]
to be unburdened, focused, gentle receivers of hospitality.
There is something about this vulnerability, about the call to
be a guest, which makes this mission so simple yet dynamic.
When I read this story I feel the vitality of the adventure that
the 72 embarked on. This is what it's like to be truly alive:
arriving as a guest, being welcomed and offering God's peace,
being consistent with your friendships, accepting generous
hospitality, bringing healing and peace and the hope of God's
Kingdom.

The flip side is that when you are not welcomed your
vulnerability as a guest is revealed. Rather than carrying the
burden of the rejection, Jesus' advice to his workers is to go
into the streets and shout:

The only thing we got from you is the dirt on our feet, and
we're giving it back. Did you have any idea that God's kingdom was right on your doorstep? (Luke 10.11–12 MSG)

How often do we carry the burden of rejection, or the shame
of lack of success? Well, Jesus' advice is clear: this is not our
responsibility; let it go; move on.

The call of Jesus is to balance out our responsibilities as
'workers for the harvest' with the call to be Jesus' unburdened
bringers of peace, healing and good news. If we do this work

---

4 Luke 10.2, translation by Tom Wright, 2004, *The Bible for
Everyone*, London: SPCK, p. 119.

obediently the hope is that we, like the returning 70, will return joyful and full of tales of the grace of God (Luke 10.17).

A restless heart finds rest in Christ[5]

'Our heart is restless', wrote Augustine, 'until it finds its rest in you.' 'God-shaped hole' is a common phrase used to describe what some understand as a fundamental human need. One indicator of what that God-shaped hole might be like is what people are looking for in bookshops. Self-help sections are generally far larger than the religion/spirituality section. It is clear, and not at all surprising, that self-esteem, anxiety and fear loom large in many people's lives. I suspect that Christianity is not often thought of as an antidote to low self-esteem. Instead, many people would think of it as contributing to, or at least encouraging, a sense of shame. We need to think about the language we use if we are to show that this is not a true picture. But it is another section of bookshops that most interests me: mindfulness. While there might be a shelf of Bibles, prayer books, and a few Christian writers in the 'Christian' section, 'Mindfulness' will take up many metres of shelving in any large bookshop.

The problem is that there isn't generally very much silence available if you go to church on a Sunday morning. But if the bookshops and interest in mindfulness is to be believed, silence, and how to be silent, is one of the greatest hungers of our time. This is a real God-shaped hole that we are not working hard enough to fill. There is a contemplative deficit in our parishes and churches. People are hungry for still-ness, for an escape from the constant chatter of our minds;

---

5 Some of this material has appeared in other forms on my blog Quodcumque (Richard Peers).

they are looking for something that is an essential part of our Christian tradition and that we are not making known to them. They want to know how, like Isaac, to find a way of meditating in the cool of the evening (Genesis 24.63), to be still as the Psalmist encourages (Psalm 46.10), to find the divine in the still small voice with Elijah (1 Kings 19.12), to go and be alone as Jesus so often did.

We are used, perhaps because of too much science fiction and ideas of time travel, to imagining that time is a straight line on which any moment could be travelled back or forward to, like points on a train track. But this is nonsense. Only *now* exists, only the present moment. It is the human mind that lives in the past, present and future. Saint Augustine, the fifth-century North African bishop, was well aware of that and wrote extensively of time and memory. Here is the former Archbishop of Canterbury Rowan Williams, in his book *On Augustine*, writing about time and memory:

> As soon as we try to think about our own acts of thinking, the spatial model is useless. The most ordinary activity of making sense – uttering a connected and intelligible sentence – is in fact quite a strange business: the syllables of a word, the words of a sentence, have to 'vanish' for the sequence to build up and do what it is meant to do. There is no meaning without this passage into *absence* because we cannot accumulate sounds without succession in language. What I am now saying, in any possible present moment, has to disappear, to fall silent and be displaced; even if I think I am repeating something, I shall have displaced one utterance by another, pushed what has just been said into silence and absence, rather than simply retrieving something that is the same. And when I do seek to retrieve what has already

been said, I face problems once again: my memory is not a territory, a space, that I can survey at a glance.

My present consciousness is bordered by drifts of sequences, half-grasped or half-recollected connections, neither wholly present nor wholly absent. Understanding myself, understanding what I am saying, involves not only speaking out what I clearly see but listening for those 'drifts', gently interrogating them. All of which leaves tantalizingly unclear just what and where the 'I' is that is doing the interrogating: it is not and cannot be a thing that stands apart from another thing called 'memory': in a crucial sense (as Augustine says explicitly), memory is what I am. The puzzle is that so much of what I am is absent from conscious awareness. To acknowledge the role of memory is to recognize that 'I' am not a simple history to be unveiled and displayed for inspection, nor a self-transparent reasoning subject. To be an intelligence in time is to be inescapably unfinished, consistently in search. I am never just 'there'. *Je est (sic) un autre*, 'I am another', might be a summary of much of Augustine's reflection in the *Confessions*.[6]

Augustine is a key influence on the author of the fourteenth-century book on the spiritual life, *The Cloud of Unknowing*. It is Augustine's teaching on the present moment that leads to the technique of prayer suggested by the author, a single, monosyllabic word repeated over and over again. The importance of that word is not the meaning but the fact that it is monosyllabic. Praying with a single syllable like this is to pray in the shortest possible interval of time, to attempt, and always to fail, to stay in the present moment. That failure is vital. It is what Rowan Williams means when he says, 'To

---

6 Williams, Rowan, 2016, *On Augustine*, London: Bloomsbury, p. 2.

be an intelligence in time is to be inescapably unfinished, consistently in search.' It is, as he puts it, a 'passage into *absence*'.[7]

It is important to be aware that *The Cloud* author does not suggest a multi-word mantra or polysyllabic word. He repeatedly insists on praying with one single, monosyllabic word. He suggests 'God' or 'Love', and using that repeatedly to batter the cloud that separates us from God. He suggests that the word be a 'dart of longing love', an arrow piercing the cloud. Later he says that it doesn't really matter what word we choose – 'sin' or 'out' would do. The most important thing is that the word must be only one syllable.

Here is the author of *The Cloud* explaining his technique for the first time:

When you apply yourself to this work, and feel by grace that you are called by God, lift up your heart to God with a humble stirring of love. And mean God who created you, and redeemed you, and who has graciously called you to this work: and admit no other thought of God. And yet not all of these, but only as it pleases you; for a bare intent directed to God is sufficient, without any other object besides himself. And if it pleases you to have this intent wrapped up and folded in a word, so that you might have a better hold on it, take just a little word of one syllable; for such a word is better than one of two syllables, for the shorter it is, the more fitting it is to the work of the spirit. And such a word is this word GOD or this word LOVE. Choose whichever of these two you wish, or another as it pleases you: whichever word you like best that is of one syllable. And fasten this

---

7 *On Augustine*, p. 2.

word to your heart, so that it is never separated from it, no matter what happens.[8]

For a couple of years now I have been using the word 'God', aloud when I can (driving, walking, in the bath etc.), and silently dropping it into my consciousness at the end of each in- and out-breath, when I can't. The rhythm, the pace, is slow. When I first started I happened to be somewhere where a neighbouring farmer was installing some fence posts, hammering them deep into the ground with a sledge hammer. The pace is similar to that and it's an image that has stuck with me, driving the word deep into my heart, the slow swing of the breath, the drawing back of the hammer and the next blow, repeating the cycle over and over again.

The author of *The Cloud* writes about 'naked intent' repeatedly. How can we have only one intention, closeness to God, piercing the cloud of unknowing and not the multiple, mixed motives that characterize us most of the time?

I don't want to make any great claims, but using this one word I have experienced something closer to 'naked intent' than I have ever experienced before. There are three reasons, I think, for this.

First, and strangely, because it is deeply unsatisfying. The single word leaves me wanting more. The constant repetition renders the word almost meaningless. Yet that emptiness, that nothingness, nonsense-ness also makes it *transparent*, so that when I come to pray with more traditional prayers it seems to complete the word, and the word seems to continue in and through the liturgy in a way not possible with a more complex phrase. The word can repeat itself throughout the worship

8 Hodgson, Phyllis (ed.), 1944, *The Cloud of Unknowing and Book of Privy Counseling*, Oxford: Early English Text Society, p. 76.

Second, one of the best ways I can think of to describe the experience is physical nakedness. Unless we are naturists we so rarely find ourselves naked in another's presence other than with a marital partner. Even the doctor normally sees only a part of us. The nakedness of the single word of prayer locking each utterance to the present moment is like the nakedness of the first sexual encounter, not the consummation, but preceding it, the exposure. The moment of utter vulnerability, of utter surprise and unknowing, mixed with delight and anticipation. We often think of sexual passion as a metaphor for our relationship with God, we all know that the Song of Songs and other biblical texts point us to that. But I wonder if, in our sex-obsessed culture, we make enough of chastity – desire examined for its own sake, enjoyed and appreciated without the need for consummation. And not just sexual desire: how about allowing ourselves the time to linger in that liminal moment of hunger without eating, of not being in control?

Third, another image for how this works is the reason, I think, the author is so insistent on the word being just one syllable. If our prayer is to enable us to experience the eternity of God's existence/presence, if the opposite of that eternal 'moment' is time passing, perhaps one way of experiencing eternity is to be totally present in just one moment, the smallest possible unit of time, the present moment; so our prayer word needs to be the shortest possible duration, one syllable, one moment. If we can focus all our attentiveness, all our own presence in that split moment, we will experience, we are experiencing, eternity. Time splits and opens us to eternity. That is travelling lightly.

'The Sacrament of the Present Moment' is the Christian tradition's gift to the desire that leads people to mindfulness. Experiencing *now* is the authenticity that Jesus brought to every moment; Jesus could do this because to experience eternity is not to experience an endless line of events, it is to experience existence in its purest form, in the now.

Far from being in opposition to or even in any way different from faith, I have come to believe that there is something about the experience of mindfulness that prepares people for faith. This has emerged in conversation with adults and children who have participated in my mindfulness training over the last 30 years. Mindfulness leads to four experiences, all of which are gateways to faith:

1 – compassion
2 – connectedness
3 – watchfulness
4 – abandonment.

Compassion

When people sit still, observe their breathing, notice their thoughts coming and going, they always experience something close to a feeling of love. They feel more loving and more loved. Although, very occasionally, distressing thoughts and memories do arise, this is really quite rare and even then it is within a larger experience of love.

Connectedness

Although mindfulness may appear to be a very solitary, individualistic exercise, focused on the self, in fact the internal experience is of being less separated and more connected, not just to people but to the physical world. Sitting still and observing the breath is a strongly physical experience. It is not 'all in the mind'.

Watchfulness

I have been undecided on what to call this experience and wondered about 'awakeness'. In the end I've decided on watchfulness because it has Christian history in the *Philokalic* tradition of Russian spirituality, where the writings of the *Philokalia*[9] are the writings of the 'neptic' ones, the 'awake', the 'watchful'. Participants typically describe this as being more alert, or even more alive. Occasionally, in the early stages and often with teenagers, there is a feeling of sleepiness; sleep deprivation is a significant problem, but this usually passes.

Abandonment

Again, I haven't been very certain what to call this. Because mindfulness is about noticing things, and particularly noticing thoughts as they arise and as they pass, it increases the ability to let go, to not need to be in control. This is very helpful preparation for abandonment to God. It is the only way I know that we can travel lightly.

Reflecting on the idea of a 'God-shaped hole' is interesting, but I am not convinced that the phrase is particularly helpful. Frankly, if there is a God-shaped hole, most people in our societies don't feel it, or the need to fill it. Rather, it seems to me that people find not a lack of something in mindfulness

---

9 Palmer, G. E. H., Sheerard, P., Ware, Kallistos (eds), 1979, *The Philokalia: The Complete Text* (4 volumes), London: Faber & Faber.

but a waking up of a very real, positive part of themselves that has been underused; this is a good biblical image too, since Jesus reminds us to 'stay awake'. When people experience compassion, connectedness, watchfulness and abandonment, they are experiencing God. This rule encourages us to travel light. Watchfulness is about lifestyle. As soon as we start to be watchful we notice things about the way we live, our sleeping, eating, working. Travelling light is more than just de-cluttering, although that can be helpful sometimes. Travelling light is an attitude to things and to time, to our lives and to our minds. It is how we live, who we are.

Tools for the toolkit

- Diary discipline:
  Be ruthless
  Say no to things.
- Have a day a week in the diary for desk things.
- Mark three separate weeks in the year when you don't make appointments. Use them for:
  Catch-up
  Reading
  Visits.
- Keep reading; never stop being interested in things.
- Have regular sleeping patterns: same time to bed, same time out of bed at least five days a week, or better still, every day.
- Don't self-medicate. Alcohol really doesn't make things better.
- Stop screen time of any sort an hour before you sleep; even 30 minutes will help.

- Avoid carbohydrates. A sugar high means a low to follow.
- Have some silent time every day. Even five minutes a day will change your life.
- Recognize the things you can control (very short list) and the things you can't. Reinhold Niebuhr's Serenity Prayer contains a lot of wisdom.

Books to read

Annan, Kent, 2016, *Slow Kingdom Coming: Practices for Doing Justice, Loving Mercy and Walking Humbly in the World*, Downers Grove, IL: IVP.

Bowler, Kate, 2018, *Everything Happens For A Reason and Other Lies I've Loved*, London: SPCK.

Cain, Susan, 2012, *Quiet*, London: Penguin Books.

Corbett, Sarah, 2017, *How to be a Craftivist: The Art of Gentle Protest*, London: Unbound.

Hodgson, Phyllis (ed.), 1944, *The Cloud of Unknowing and Book of Privy Counseling*, Oxford: Early English Text Society.

Julian of Norwich, 2015, *Revelations of Divine Love*, Oxford: Oxford University Press.

Kabat-Zinn, John, 2013, *Full Catastrophe Living*, London: Piatkus.

Laird, Martin, 2006, *Into the Silent Land*, London: Darton, Longman and Todd.

Nouwen, Henri, 1996, *Reaching Out*, London: Fount.

Palmer, G. E. H., Sheerard, P., Ware, Kallistos (eds), 1979, *The Philokalia: The Complete Text* (4 volumes), London: Faber & Faber.

Pema, Chödrön, 2007, *When Things Fall Apart*, Rockport, MA: Element Books.

Pliny the Elder, *Natural History*, translated by Harris Rackham, Loeb, 1950, Book XIX, Chapter LIV.

Rohr, Richard, 2014, *A Lever and a Place to Stand: The Contemplative Stance, the Active Prayer*, Mahwah, NJ: Paulist Press.

Thorne, Brian, 2003, *Infinitely Beloved: The Challenge of Divine Intimacy*, London: Darton, Longman and Todd.

Tyler, Peter, 2018, *Christian Mindfulness*, London: SCM Press.

Williams, Rowan, 2016, *On Augustine*, London: Bloomsbury.

Useful websites

Windmind, www.wildmind.org.

Breathworks Mindfulness, www.breathworks-mindfulness.org.uk.

World Community for Christian Meditation, www.wccm.org.

Craftivist Collective, https://craftivist-collective.com/.

The Corrymeela Community, www.corrymeela.org/.

The Iona Community, https://iona.org.uk/.

Fr Richard Peers Blogs, https://oikodomeo.home.blog (see also https://educationpriest.wordpress.com).

Serenity Prayer, www.celebraterecovery.com/resources/cr-tools/serenityprayer.

Rule #12

Tell Stories

This is a true story this is

St Luke the Evangelist Church sits on the corner of City Road and Gwladys Street in Walton, Liverpool. Next to the church is the Gwladys Street Stand of Goodison Park, home to Everton Football Club. Next to the football stadium is Gwladys Street School. Built around the time of both the church and the club, the school is a hive of activity and, as a community school in an area that has a number of social challenges, it provides a great deal more than just a good education for the children of Walton. During my time as vicar in the parish I also served as a governor of the school and would visit them at least once a week. One of my favourite things to do when I visited was to tell the children stories from the Bible. Rather like a good old-fashioned Sunday school teacher, I would tell them the story of David and Goliath, Daniel in the lion's den, Joseph and his coat of many colours, Ruth and Naomi, Noah's Ark and so on; and if there was a song to accompany the story, we would learn it.

These story times would usually last about 20 minutes and I would ask them to tell their own stories around the themes of the Bible stories. They might then draw pictures or the older ones write a story of their own. Anyway, one day I had a phone call from school asking a favour – Year

Two had won 'class of the week' because they had 100 per cent attendance. This meant that they were allowed to choose a class treat for the following week. Apparently after some debate they had decided that what they wanted was 'Ellen to come and tell the story about the tower again'. I don't mind telling you that I was so pleased and honoured to be asked that I nearly cried (and obviously I remain very proud of this, otherwise I wouldn't be telling you!). They had chosen a Bible story above pizza, own clothes and Friday afternoon games. It was one of the proudest moments of my ministry.

This group of children loved the story of the Tower of Babel. They knew all the twists and turns, they understood the consequences of hubris,[1] they imaged the height of the tower and were able to tell me exactly what it was made of. They listed a great number of languages that emerged after God split us up and even made up a language that we all had before the tower. The story was a source of what seemed like endless fascination to them – and you should see the pictures they drew of that tower!

The stories that we are equipped to tell, the stories of the people of God and the grace of God in the Old and New Testament of the Bible and the gospel stories being lived out in our own lives: these are the richest source of hope that we have. Even in the complexity and contradiction of the stories we tell, the truth of God's justice and mercy emerges. Telling the good news of Jesus Christ afresh in the world today is what we are called to do as Christian activists. We do this in word and deed: telling our stories, bringing hope and sharing love.

This chapter is a bit different from the others in that the writer, the community theologian and social activist Ann

---

1 Excessive pride towards or defiance of the gods, leading to downfall, particularly in Greek tragedy.

Morisy, explores something of her thinking about how stories work, their importance to us culturally and how they
impact our lives and our understanding of our discipleship.
But first some Bible thinking from me.

Scattering and gathering

Now the whole world had one language and a common
speech. As people moved eastward, they found a plain in
Shinar and settled there.

They said to each other, 'Come, let's make bricks and bake
them thoroughly.' They used brick instead of stone, and
bitumen for mortar. Then they said, 'Come, let us build
ourselves a city, with a tower that reaches to the heavens, so
that we may make a name for ourselves; otherwise we will
be scattered over the face of the whole earth.'

But the LORD came down to see the city and the tower
the people were building. The LORD said, 'If as one people speaking the same language they have begun to do this,
then nothing they plan to do will be impossible for them.
Come, let us go down and confuse their language so they
will not understand each other.'

So the LORD scattered them from there over all the earth,
and they stopped building the city. That is why it was called
Babel – because there the LORD confused the language of
the whole world. From there the LORD scattered them over
the face of the whole earth. (Genesis 11.1–9 NIV)

When the day of Pentecost had come, they were all together
in one place. And suddenly from heaven there came a
sound like the rush of a violent wind, and it filled the entire house where they were sitting. Divided tongues, as of

fire, appeared among them, and a tongue rested on each of them. All of them were filled with the Holy Spirit and began to speak in other languages, as the Spirit gave them ability. Now there were devout Jews from every nation under heaven living in Jerusalem. And at this sound the crowd gathered and was bewildered, because each one heard them speaking in the native language of each. Amazed and astonished, they asked, 'Are not all these who are speaking Galileans? And how is it that we hear, each of us, in our own native language? Parthians, Medes, Elamites, and residents of Mesopotamia, Judea and Cappadocia, Pontus and Asia, Phrygia and Pamphylia, Egypt and the parts of Libya belonging to Cyrene, and visitors from Rome, both Jews and proselytes, Cretans and Arabs – in our own languages we hear them speaking about God's deeds of power.' (Acts 2.1–11)

I am not very good at communicating verbally when I go abroad. I don't speak any language (other than English) well – I can barely get by in French and know a few words of German. It is a great frustration to me as I am a conversationalist. I love to hear people's stories, hear news, share ideas, play about with words. When I am out of my comfort zone with language I feel lost and like a fish out of water. This feeling goes beyond purely language issues – if I don't understand a culture I also feel frustrated. If I don't get what people mean when they are using slang, or street talk; if there are particular cultural references that I miss, I feel disappointed. In the same way, if I don't share a common history with people, if I don't know about place names, where streets are, who lived where and so on, I feel out of the loop and a bit out of place.

You see, language – our understanding of words, our cultural references, the way we talk to each other – is tied up with our sense of being and our identities. The words we use, the things we talk about help us to belong. They also help us to be able to identify those people who don't belong: the words we use enable us to separate ourselves from people who are different; our language divides us into those who are like us and those who are 'other'.

These two passages, one from the Old Testament and the other from the New Testament, tell us something of the way God views language. In these stories we see how language separates human beings from each other and how it has the capacity to unite. The Tower of Babel is not only a warning to human beings to make sure they don't think they are better than God but also a story in which the goodness of God and mercy of God are demonstrated.

In Genesis 1.28, God tells human beings to 'live all over the earth' (GNB). It is God's intention that human beings should populate the earth and not stick together. What strikes me in Genesis 11.4 is that these people don't want to be 'scattered'. They don't want to do what God has asked them to do. They want to stay the same, do the same things and stay close to each other. Yet again this is a story about people going directly against what God has asked them to do. So what do they decide to do? They decide to build a tower to protect themselves against God's instructions. Indeed, it's worse than that. They don't just want to cling together, they build with the intention of becoming like God! They build a city and a tower to exclude God – and not just to keep God out but to keep themselves in.

This desire to be one homogenous unit goes against God's plan. This isn't what God had in mind. God appears to have intended us to be diverse, to scatter – to populate the world God created. So what we have here is a story about people resisting God's plan for diversity and then God insisting on diversity. Because when the Lord comes down to take a look at what these people had been doing, it becomes horribly apparent that yet again human beings – God's people – have been disobedient. By not scattering they have become a very strong force against God; they have built a fortress against God's plans and have become united in their disobedience. Theirs is a typical 'fortress mentality'. Together these people are in danger of self-destructing.

So do we see God's actions here as punishment or an act of salvation? What do you think?

Well, I think it is both. God *has* to scatter these people, because if they don't disperse they will destroy themselves and are in danger of creating a wedge between themselves and God. God has to save them by splitting them up. But for these people their vanity has to be well and truly put to rest. They can't be given any way to return to this folly. Until final salvation is secured, people cannot ever be in danger of uniting against God again. So the scattering of people physically and the scattering of people's language is a way of helping God's people not to make the same mistakes again. Walter Brueggemann describes this story as 'a protest against every effort at oneness derived from human self-sufficiency and autonomy'.[2]

So does that mean that we should avoid uniting – just in case we get it wrong again? Should we play it safe and not communicate with other races, nations and tribes? Just stick to people like us who speak the same language, have the same accent, have the same cultural references? Well, of course not. If we do that we are just building mini towers of Babel – all we are doing is maintaining our own 'fortress mentality' against other people. What God expects from the diversity God has

2 Walter Brueggemann, 1982, *Genesis: Interpretation: A Bible Commentary*, Louisville KY: John Knox Press, p. 100.

willed is that the world should be, as Walter Brueggemann suggests: 'organized for God's purposes of joy, delight, freedom, doxology, and caring. Such a world must partake of the *unity God wills* and the *scattering God envisions*.'[3] We must avoid one-dimensional views of either God's unity or scattering.

As we heard in our second reading from Acts, on the day of Pentecost God blessed the people with the ability to understand each other. But they didn't stop being people from many nations; they didn't have to give up their cultural identity to be understood by each other. God gave them this gift as a sign of their unity in Christ. It didn't cost them their nationhood. They carried on being people who were identifiably from 'Parthia, Media, and Elam; from Mesopotamia, Judea, and Cappadocia; from Pontus and Asia, from Phrygia and Pamphylia, from Egypt and the regions of Libya near Cyrene [and also] Rome' (GNB). The Word of God blows over their chaos and gives them the ability to see themselves, hear themselves, understand themselves as the people of God over and above their identity as people of a named nation, tribe or race.

We can see that 'the breaking of language at Babel is deep'.[4] In our society we live with the consequences of not understanding, not hearing, not listening to our international neighbours. Even on a domestic level this broken understanding divides us city from city, neighbourhood from neighbourhood, gang from gang, clique from clique. Even with the hope of Pentecost we still long for the time when nation will unite with nation and we will be able to speak and listen to each other without misunderstanding, violence or struggle. It is a longed-for promise that we have to continue to reach out for as Christians and do all we can to heal the nations. For most of us who don't

3 Brueggemann, *Genesis*, p. 101; emphasis original.
4 Brueggemann, *Genesis*, p. 104.

have opportunities to participate in international relations, we must be content to work at unity here at home – by healing rifts in personal relationships, working through our misunderstandings, celebrating our diversity and finding ways to share ideas and finding common language, and above all listening to each other. But all the time we should remember the lesson from this story of the Tower of Babel and not attempt to build edifices that hide us from God, that shut God out or make us feel more important than God. As Matthew the Gospel writer says: '[We] are like light for the whole world. A city built on a hill cannot be hid' (5.14 GNB).

Activism + story-rich life = discipleship

Ann Morisy, the writer and social activist, makes a number of points that are relevant to our rules for social action. The first point is that when we involve ourselves in 'struggle', to use that honoured description of social action, we gain a host of enlivening stories – we become story rich. The second point is that the stories that surround us shape our imagination – for good or for ill. The third point is that stories, more than facts alone, motivate us to change things – in our lives and in the world. And finally, stories are an example of abundance: stories can be shared in the telling and they lose nothing in the process; stories can be retold by other people and can spread far and wide – and lose nothing in the process. And at their very heart stories carry an invitation: stories in the telling say to others 'You can come too.'

Ann Morisy writes:

An old priest friend once said that he had never been stuck for a sermon since the day centre for homeless people had opened in his church. This was because he had become story rich. The stories he heard from the homeless people had a quality that stuck with him – stories that went down deep and lit up the Gospels for him, and lit up his preaching. The stories that he heard combined hope and hardship, and often acts of exceptional generosity and dignity. These are the stories we rub up against when we embrace the challenge of social activism, and we too will likely find that the Gospels come alive for us because such stories act by incarnation, they give flesh and life to what too easily could be just abstract and academic.

Try this story:

My old Mum, Peg, worked all her life in a local shop. At Christmas things would get very busy as people came for the items they had asked to be put aside for them until they had saved up enough in the Christmas club the shop ran each year. On Christmas Eve my Mum came home late and exhausted, which was to be expected. But she was also upset. The owner of the shop had informed her that the till was 'out' by £20. Way back in the 1960s that was a big sum. I remember my Dad comforting my Mum by saying that he would give £20 to the owner to cover the shortfall. Nevertheless it took the wind out of our sails that Christmas.

When the shop opened up after the Christmas break, at mid-morning in comes one of the regulars: Dolly Woolly. Dolly was one of the poorest people in a very poor neighbourhood. She was thin and stooped and her mac had faded with age. She had two school-aged children who would have had a lean Christmas. She beckoned my Mum to one side, 'Peg, look, I found this £20 note in with the bits and pieces I'd got with my Christmas-club money ...'

Let me list what that story has given me:

- A deep awareness of how dignity and self-denying honesty are exhibited by many who get by on very little.

- An inclination to think deeply to hold off the desire to snatch at any largesse that might come my way.
- A deep respect for my Mum, who gave her heart and soul to her work in that little shop on Hawthorn Road in Bootle.
- A deep appreciation of a Gospel that is full of stories in which those who have least understand and act in exceptional ways.
- An opportunity to say thank you to Dolly Woolly, who lived a lowly life dogged by hardship – and was often scorned by those who didn't realize she also wore a crown.

In sharing that story with you I have issued an invitation: 'You come too.' And in this invitation resides the formative and healing power of stories. In recalling and writing the story I took great care to make sure that you got not just the gist but could also engage with details, perhaps even create a mental image of this event that took place when I was a youngster. In telling you this story I have handed it over to you; it is now your story as well as mine, and you can do with it as you wish. Stories are given and exchanged – and in the process lose nothing of their potency; story is like 'currency' because, just like money, story can change hands and lose no value in the process.

William James, the nineteenth-century philosopher and psychologist, observed that the greatest gap that exists in the universe is that between one human mind and another. Story is our best hope for flying over the chasms that separate individuals, ethnicity, genders, ages (and ages) and the myriad other differences that have grown exponentially in a globalizing world. Story is a counter to Babel. Story – personal stories – enables us to see and understand the messy particulars that make us act as we do. Stories change how we see people. For example, to return to the priest I referred to at the outset, he had discovered that some of those whom he met were indeed contemplatives and well formed in their relationship and confidence with God. No longer could he impose stereotypes on those who slept on the streets. He had changed, and perhaps the homeless people to whom he had given time and effort to listen to their stories had also changed.

Most of us can rise no higher than the stories that surround us. Stories, like mother's milk, are filled with nutrients from which lives grow – but stuff that we absorb with our mothers' milk can be problematic; it needs to be recognized for its limitations. Paulo Freire, an adult educator from Brazil, urges people to develop a critical consciousness that can scrutinize the stories that have gone deep into our consciousness and shape the way we act and think. He calls this process of rigorous and honest reflection 'conscientization'. Jesus had to discover this. And he discovered it the hard way.

Let me remind you of the story: this story with slight variation is told in both Matthew's Gospel, chapter 15 and Mark's Gospel, chapter 7. And often it fills the preacher and even the theologian with dread, because it shows Jesus in an unusually harsh light; and if we are really frank, it depicts Jesus acting in a racist way.

Jesus and his disciples moved to the coastal region of Tyre. One gets the impression that he and the disciples were seeking a bit of a break after their bruising ministry in Galilee. Their aim was to enjoy some anonymity. But to everyone's frustration, a woman arrived insisting that Jesus heal her daughter. The disciples urged Jesus to send her away because she kept shouting and making such a commotion, they feared their cover might be blown.

Her nuisance level reached such a peak that when she was eventually allowed to see Jesus, he gave her verbal abuse. He called her a dog because she wasn't a Jew, and he said his ministry was first and foremost to the Jews 'It is not fair to take the children's food and throw it to the dogs', said Jesus, and this mother, perhaps the only person in the Gospels to use repartee to engage, replied, 'Yes, Lord, yet even the dogs eat the crumbs that fall from their masters' table.' And we read that Jesus responded, 'Woman, great is your faith! Let it be done for you as you wish'. And when that mother returned home she found her daughter healed (Matthew 15.26–28).

The main debate about this story usually focuses on Jesus' understanding that his ministry to the Gentiles would only take place after the Jews, his own people, had accepted him as messiah. Other theologians have concentrated on trying to minimize the offensiveness of Jesus' language to this mother. The term 'dog', even today, is the supreme insult in the east. Biblical scholars are quick to point out that the Greek in which the Gospel was written doesn't use the term 'dogs', but rather a word that could be translated as puppies. This would turn the encounter between Jesus and the woman into something more akin to friendly banter.

However, we have to scotch this because Jesus' original words would have been spoken in his native tongue: Aramaic – and Aramaic does not have a linguistic form that corresponds with the word pups and puppies.

Jesus called the woman a dog and we have to square this racial abuse that Jesus hands out to this non-Jewish woman with the fundamental assumption that Jesus lived his life on earth without sin. The options appear to be stark: either racial abuse is not a sin or Jesus did commit a sin. But there is an honest way of resolving this paradox and it highlights the importance of developing a critical consciousness that can scrutinize the stories that have become embedded in our consciousness and shape the way we act and think.

Jesus, in calling the woman a dog, was thinking and acting

on the basis of the stories and notions he had absorbed as child and youth. He, like everyone, had been conditioned to think in particular ways. As the Son of God, born of Mary and living as a Jew in Nazareth, he could do no other than think and act as a Jew. None of us can escape the limitations imposed by the stories and notions that are poured into us by the culture into which we are born. Jesus thought and acted as a Jew when he was confronted by this persistent mother. It is not a sin to have thoughts and attitudes that are a product of our cultural background. We can do no other than interpret the world with the concept our culture provides.

If we can face the fact that Jesus was racially abusive to this Greek mother, then we can understand the importance of interrogating the stories and notions that shape our thinking and actions. Jesus, by the grace of God, was engaged by this mother's refusal to trade insults with him or to be deferential when confronted by elitist Judaism. Perhaps the sin that Jesus risked was to refuse the opportunity for dialogue with this foreign woman passionately concerned for her daughter. If Jesus had refused to enter into dialogue, he would have missed the insight that she uncovered for him. Jesus was prepared to be changed by the passionate commitment of this Greek mother, and his acceptance of this Gentile woman represents the moment in the Gospel where Jesus acknowledges that his mission is as much to the Gentiles as it is to the Jews.

It is through dialogue, especially with those who have different life experiences from our own, that we embark on the process of conscientization. At the heart of dialogue is openness to the possibility of being changed by the testimony – or the story – of another person or group. Dialogue, the willingness to see things differently, does not necessarily require long discussions and heart-searching; it can happen in a momentary encounter, as it did for Jesus. However, that moment of insight resonates throughout a lifetime and transforms the cluster of values that made us who we once were.

Jesus was willing to be changed by this experience, he was prepared to dialogue and he began to scrutinize ideas and thoughts that he had taken for granted. That moment of insight triggered by the repartee of a Gentile woman resonated through Jesus' life. From this point on we find Jesus asking questions rather than making statements. We find Jesus making his ministry to women a priority, a commitment and practice that was completely at odds with his culture and time. For Jesus, that moment of insight in Tyre resonated throughout his lifetime and transformed the cluster of values that he had inherited from his context and culture.

Stories of encounters and experiences that carry powerful, life-changing insights I refer to as generative stories. I shared with you the story of Dolly Woolly and listed for you how this encounter had had an impact on how I saw the world. Generative stories are the lifeblood of social activism because a positive feedback loop is created: a story moves to engage and connect and to discover a passionate commitment, which in turn exposes us to more stories that energize and transform. Generative stories, much better than reason, energize ethical behaviour. No matter how much our heads know, if our hearts are not persuaded, we are not convinced – and certainly not enough to act.

Generative stories are those that:

- Engage us wholly, including our emotions
- Are specific to each person; that is, they represent a person's unique encounter or pattern of encounters
- Have the capacity to become a building block of a person's identity because they provide a new way of seeing and understanding

- Often have the themes of both hope and struggle at the heart of the story
- Carry an imperative to make some kind of response, either consciously or unconsciously, because generative stories can go very deep and their impact may not be obvious
- Have an emotional potency that will likely provoke pondering and reflection as we try to integrate the experience or story into our value system.

At this point it is important to stress that stories, like any powerful phenomenon, have the capacity for both good and for ill. Poverty, mental illness, abuse, witnessing violence, all carry the risk of overwhelming experiences. To have a life that is marked by stories of being overwhelmed has a profound impact on the body's stress-managing systems. It is one thing to have a single event that knocks you back, but what if the knock-backs come thick and fast? Facing multiple overwhelmings is bound to make us wary, anxious and distrustful, and such adversity gets under the skin.

Jesus challenges the man who had lingered at the side of the pool at Bethesda for years and years. Even though the man was healed by his encounter with Jesus, he was healed in body but retained a spirit of resentment, causing trouble for Jesus by telling the Jewish leaders that Jesus had healed him on the Sabbath (John 5.1–18).

Most of us figure out how to live safely within a given set of social rules, ensuring that our lives are maintained at a low level of intensity, avoiding being pulled off balance by threatening or challenging experiences. There is no blame attached to this; after all, we know all too well how we are vulnerable, paradoxically creative and yet helpless creatures – with an intimation that we are special. Mostly we need to be coaxed and enticed if we are to stick our neck out. For most of us, our social action needs an *amenable gradient*. Mostly we are not heroes, but need some structure that supports our participation. Mostly our social action will involve encounters within bounds that give reassurance that we won't be overwhelmed, even though our context is one in which we will have little power. Nevertheless we will encounter stories that will:

- Alter our view of the world
- Help us rethink how we fit into that world
- Place us in situations that resonate precisely with the stories we know about Jesus.

Your stories are as important as all the other stories because you are good news

The 'great commission' of Jesus is that we need to tell our stories, tell the story of Jesus, and tell the story of God's people – of all that is good in the world:

> And Jesus came and said to them, 'All authority in heaven and on earth has been given to me. Go therefore and make disciples of all nations, baptizing them in the name of the Father and of the Son and of the Holy Spirit, and teaching them to obey everything that I have commanded you. And remember, I am with you always, to the end of the age.' (Matthew 28.18–20)

Ann Morisy is a great encourager and she is a good teacher. She often tells me that the stories I tell need to be told better. Ann pushes me to go deeper into the point I want to make, to frame it more beautifully, to ask harder questions, to share more of myself. This is because when I tell my story well, when it is the truth about me, it is the story of Jesus. When I tell the stories of other people well, when it is the truth about them, it is the story of Jesus. These stories are not static, stuck in history or confined to a single place. These are dynamic, transforming stories and each of us is slap-bang in the middle of it – the greatest story ever told. This is our story, God's story, the story of God's son Jesus and the wisdom of the Holy Spirit. This story is not going away.

This final rule is probably the most important rule of all. Stories matter. You must keep on telling them.

Tools for the toolkit

- Facts aren't important but you *must* tell the truth.
- The fruit of the spirit is: love, joy, peace, patience, kindness, generosity, faithfulness, gentleness and self-control (see Galatians 5.22–23). It is worth bearing in mind that if your stories are not fruitful they might not be worth telling. Avoid stories that tell that you hurt people.
- Be the story yourself: let other people tell your story and listen because it is probably a lot more encouraging than you think.
- Some stories are hard to tell and not all stories have happy endings: they still might be important and need to be heard.
- There a lot of ways to tell a story: poetry, narrative, fiction, autobiography, biography and so on. Mess about with style and content. Enjoy the form.

- Always ask questions about the stories you are told. Be suspicious and find out why you are being told this story at this point and in this way.
- Let stories change you – you are free to be whoever you want to be, so allow yourself to be changed by the big story of God's love.

Books to read

Borg, Marcus J., 1994, *Meeting Jesus Again for the First Time: The Historical Jesus and the Heart of Contemporary Faith*, New York: HarperCollins Publishers.

Dillon, Christine, 2012, *Telling the Gospel Through Story*, Downers Grove, IL: IVP.

Eagleton, Terry, 2007, *The Gospels: Jesus Christ (Revolutions)*, London: Verso.

Fee, Gordon D.; Douglas Stuart, 1982, *How to Read the Bible for All It's Worth*, Grand Rapids, MI: Academie Books.

Havel, Vaclav, 1990, *Letters to Olga: June 1979 to September 1982*, London: Faber & Faber.

Morisy, Ann, 1997, *Beyond the Good Samaritan: Community Ministry and Mission*, London: Continuum.

——, 2011, *Borrowing from the Future: A Faith-based Approach to Intergenerational Equity*, London: Continuum.

Conclusion

Taking Part in Massive Change

> We each have the power to inspire. To inspire we
> must do two things: first, be open to possibility.
> Second, live with purpose and ideals.[1]

Just one more story before I finish.

I met Bruce Mau in 2010 when he came to work in West
Everton in Liverpool. He was invited, as part of the 2010
Year of Health and Wellbeing, to kick-start a programme
that would 'act as an engine to instigate massive change in
the social, civic, health, and creative cultures of the people
of North Liverpool'. This was a big vision and a 'big ask' of
a small beleaguered community weary of outsiders coming
in to 'help'. Nevertheless, we took the risk, and that hot
summer's day the big man from New York was squashed into
a small room in the West Everton Community Council building, along with about 20 local activists and artists, to start in
a small way the massive change.

Bruce started to talk about design – about how we are all
surrounded by design and that if we don't design our own
world somebody will design it for us.

---

1 Mau, Bruce, 2015, *Design is Leadership*, Massive Change Network, available from https://static1.squarespace.com/static/579eod
66cd0f685ac1c2a761/t/57dc3fd3d482e9d2d55e8ad8/14740
52055871/24hrs2mc-Principles.pdf (accessed 3 February 2020).

He said: we build brands from the inside out.[2]

So there we were building our brand. From the inside out. One (sound)bite at a time.

The next day Polly Mosely had organized a day for us all to be on the park 'building our brand', asking questions like: What sort of park did we want for the future? What was it for? Who was it for? Did we want housing or a green space? Did we want a piece of iconic art? Did we need a café? What about toilets?

We sat in a large pink tepee drinking tea and eating home-made scouse and cakes, looking out over the city and the Mersey estuary, telling the man from New York about the ruins of the houses that were under our feet, the money spent by Militant to build 'the people's park', the fight for social housing and the displacement of a community. We talked about how proud we are of the views and the wonderful undulating 'telly-tubby' mound design of the park. We sang songs and laughed a lot. We realized our brand was us – the people, the community centres, the churches, the shops, the pubs, the disfunction and the muddle, the celebration and the joy – we are Everton Park. By the end of the day we were 'on purpose'. We had a plan to look after the park, to celebrate it whenever we could and to ensure that it remained a green space open for all.

I am telling you this story because it was Bruce Mau, and his ideas about what he calls 'Massive Change',[3] that helped me see that I need to be more focused about how I live and work as a Christian. I need to be 'on purpose', setting bound-aries, laying down my own rules for life, so that there is no room for other people, or systems, to creep in and design my life for me. My life is framed by my faith and this is the

---

2 www.brucemaudesign.com/.

3 Mau, Bruce, 2004, *Massive Change*, London: Phaidon Press.

boundary within which I want to live. This becomes possible through the Spirit of God, who inspires and focuses that vision, and it is laid out in the pattern of the life of Christ.

Massive change happens for us when we start to take seriously the call of God and begin to be moulded into the person God has called us to be. When we let the small things join up they make a massive change in us that leads to a shift in conscious thought and behaviour. Being a Christian activist is about consciously joining the dots God has dotted out for us and then prayerfully cracking on with being the best human we possibly can be. Changing the world for the better is first and foremost about flourishing as we were designed by God to be, then enabling others to flourish.

So what kind of world do we want to live in? What kind of world did God design for us?

I think the world God designed for us is full of justice and mercy, a land of fairness and gentleness, a place where people are free and thrive, a country overflowing with generosity. This is a great design, isn't it? This is God's design and we need to work up that design and start living it. Nothing less will do. God's kingdom on earth as it is in heaven.

I pray that this book has inspired you to be an active participant in the designing of your life according to God's magnificent plan. I pray that you will make up your own rules for Christian activism (you're welcome to use mine but the ones you design for yourself, and the stories you will tell of your extraordinary life, will be better!). Being a courageous follower of Christ, being an activist in God's kingdom plan, this is the best design for life that I can possibly commend to you.

Brothers and sisters, enjoy the adventure.

I am going to leave the last word to Jesus:

Go therefore and make disciples of all nations, baptizing
them in the name of the Father and of the Son and of the
Holy Spirit, and teaching them to obey everything that I
have commanded you. And remember, I am with you
always, to the end of the age. (Matthew 28.19–20)

Books to read

Beadle, Phil, 2017, *Rules for Mavericks: A Manifesto for Dissident Creatives*, Carmarthen: Crown House Publishing.

Bonino, José Míguez, 1983, *Toward a Christian Political Ethics*,
London: SCM Press.

Bryant, Chris, 1996, *Possible Dreams: A Personal History of the
British Christian Socialists*, London: Hodder & Stoughton.

Holmes, Lucy-Anne, 2015, *How to Start a Revolution*, London:
Transworld.

Huxley, Justine Afra, 2019, *Generation Y, Spirituality and Social
Change*, London: Jessica Kingsley.

Mau, Bruce, 2004, *Massive Change*, London: Phaidon Press.

Oakley, Nigel, 2007, *Engaging Politics? The Tensions of Christian
Political Involvement*, Milton Keynes: Paternoster.

Pearce, Nick; Paxton, Will, 2005, *Social Justice: Building a Fairer
Britain*, London: Politico's Publishing.

Peterson, Jordan B., 2018, *12 Rules for Life: An Antidote to
Chaos*, London: Penguin Random House.

Popovic, Srdja; Millar, Matthew, 2015, *Blueprint for Revolution:
How to Use Rice Pudding, Lego Men, and Other Non-Violent
Techniques to Galvanise Communities, Overthrow Dictators,
or Simply Change the World*, London: Scribe.

Rawls, John, 2001, *Justice as Fairness: A Restatement*, Cambridge, MA: Harvard University Press.

Ricketts, Aidan, 2012, *The Activists' Handbook: A Step-by-step
Guide to Participatory Democracy*, London: Zed Books.

Segalov, Michael, 2018, *Resist! How to be an Activist in the Age
of Defiance*, London: Laurence King.

Shaw, Randy, 1996, *The Activist's Handbook: A Primer*, London:
University of California Press.

Activist equipment

- Tea and coffee: I might also suggest bread, butter and a toaster because in my experience toast has been significant in feeding activism.
- Permanent markers: it is important to commit to action. Write it down, get it done.
- The internet: you will need to commit to social networking, writing and reading articles and writing a blog. Join in creative, joyous activism online but keep it positive and edifying.
- Notebooks: write every day. Write about anything and everything. Take notes on your experiences and your thoughts.
- Bible: whether you want an old-fashioned black floppy Bible or an app on your phone, keep a Bible handy.
- Friends and comrades – brothers and sisters in Christ: get a group of people together regularly to discuss politics, social action, church matters, tricky issues and so on; a trusted group of people you can be brave with and speak boldly about the things that matter.

Bibliography

Ahern, Geoffrey, 1987, *Inner City God: The Nature of Belief in the Inner City*, London: Hodder & Stoughton.

Akala, 2019, *Natives: Race and Class in the Ruins of Empire*, London: Two Roads.

Alinsky, Saul D., 1971, *Rules for Radicals: A Pragmatic Primer for Realistic Radicals*, New York: Vintage Books.

Alker, Adrian, 2016, *Is a Radical Church Possible?*, Alresford: Christian Alternative Books.

Annan, Kent, 2016, *Slow Kingdom Coming: Practices for Doing Justice, Loving Mercy and Walking Humbly in the World*, Downers Grove, IL: IVP.

Ballard, Paul; Husselbee, Lesley, 2007, *Community and Ministry: An Introduction to Community Development in a Christian Context*, London: SPCK.

Ballard, Paul; Pritchard, John, 1996, *Practical Theology in Action: Christian Thinking in the Service of Church and Society*, London: SPCK.

Bartley, Jonathan, 2006, *Faith and Politics after Christendom: The Church as a Movement for Anarchy*, Milton Keynes: Paternoster Press.

Bauckham, Richard, 2003, *Bible and Mission: Christian Witness in a Postmodern World*, Milton Keynes: Paternoster Press.

Bayes, Paul, 2019, *The Table: Knowing Jesus: Prayer, Friendship, Justice*, London: Darton, Longman and Todd.

Beadle, Phil, 2017, *Rules for Mavericks: A Manifesto for Dissident Creatives*, Carmarthen: Crown House Publishing.

Beasley-Murray, Paul, 1992, *Radical Believers: The Baptist Way of Being the Church*, Wallingford: Baptist Union of Great Britain.

Beckford, Robert, 2004, *God and the Gangs*, London: Darton, Longman and Todd.

Beeching, Vicky, 2017, *Undivided: Coming Out, Becoming Whole, and Living Free From Shame*, London: Collins.

Berry, Thomas, 1991, *Befriending the Earth: A Theology of Reconciliation Between Humans and the Earth*, Mystic, CT: Twenty-Third Publications.

Betts, Alexander; Collier, Paul, 2018, *Refuge: Transforming a Broken Refugee System*, London: Allen Lane.

Boff, Leonardo; Boff, Clodovis, 1987, *Introducing Liberation Theology*, Tunbridge Wells: Burns & Oates/Search Press.

Bond, Becky; Exley, Zack, 2016, *Rules for Revolutionaries: How Big Organizing Can Change Everything*, White River Junction, VT: Chelsea Green Publishing.

Bonhoeffer, Dietrich, 2015, *The Cost of Discipleship*, new edition, London: SCM Press.

Bonino, José Míguez, 1983, *Toward a Christian Political Ethics*, London: SCM Press.

Bookless, Dave, 2010, *God Doesn't do Waste: Redeeming the Whole of Life*, London: IVP.

Borg, Marcus J., 1994, *Meeting Jesus Again for the First Time: The Historical Jesus and the Heart of Contemporary Faith*, New York: HarperCollins.

Bowler, Kate, 2018, *Everything Happens for a Reason and Other Lies I've Loved*, London: SPCK.

Bradford, Louise, 2019, *Save the World: There is No Planet B: Things You Can Do Right Now to Save Our Planet*, London: Summersdale.

British and Foreign Bible Society, 2017, *Calling People of Goodwill: The Bible and the Common Good*, Swindon: Bible Society Resources.

Brown, Malcolm; Chaplin, Jonathan; Hughes, John; Rowlands, Anna; Suggate, Alan, 2014, *Anglican Social Theology: Renewing the Vision Today*, London: Church House Publishing.

Brueggemann, Walter, 2001, *Hope for the World: Mission in a Global Context*, Louisville, KY: Westminster John Knox Press.

——, 2011, *Subversive Obedience: Truth-Telling and the Art of Preaching*, London: SCM Press.

——, 2014, *Sabbath as Resistance: Saying No to the Culture of Now*, Louisville, KY: Westminster John Knox Press.

Bryant, Chris, 1996, *Possible Dreams: A Personal History of the British Christian Socialists*, London: Hodder & Stoughton.

Buehner, Carl W., cited by Richard L. Evans, 1971, *Richard Evans' Quote Book*, Salt Lake City, UT: Publishers Press.

Cain, Susan, 2012, *Quiet*, London: Penguin.

Charlesworth, Martin; Williams, Natalie, 2014, *The Myth of the Undeserving Poor: A Christian Response to Poverty in Britain Today*, Surrey: Grosvenor House Publishing.

Chester, Tim, 2012, *Unreached: Growing Churches in Working-class and Deprived Areas*, Nottingham: IVP.

Chödrön, Pema, 2007, *When Things Fall Apart*, Rockport, MA: Element Books.

Claiborne, Shane, 2006, *The Irresistible Revolution: Living as an Ordinary Radical*, Grand Rapids, MI: Zondervan.

Clawson, Julie, 2009, *Everyday Justice Paperback: The Global Impact of Our Daily Choices*, London: IVP.

Corbett, Sarah, 2017, *How to be a Craftivist: The Art of Gentle Protest*, London: Unbound.

Davey, Andrew, 2010, *Crossover City: Resources for Urban Mission and Transformation*, London: Mowbray.

Dillon, Christine, 2012, *Telling the Gospel through Story*, Downers Grove, IL: IVP.

Dwyer, Judith (ed.), *The New Dictionary of Catholic Social Thought*, Collegeville, MN: Liturgical Press.

Eagleton, Terry, 2007, *The Gospels: Jesus Christ (Revolutions)*, London: Verso.

Eastman, Michael; Latham, Steve, 2004, *Urban Church: A Practitioner's Resource Book*, London: SPCK.

Eddo-Lodge, Reni, 2018, *Why I'm No Longer Talking to White People About Race*, London: Bloomsbury.

Edman, Liz, 2017, *Queer Virtue: What LGBTQ People Know about Life and Love and How it Can Revitalize Christianity*, Boston, MA: Beacon Press.

Fee, Gordon D.; Douglas Stuart, 1982, *How to Read the Bible for All it's Worth*, Grand Rapids, MI: Academie Books.

Filby, Eliza, 2015, *God and Mrs Thatcher: The Battle for Britain's Soul*, London: Biteback.

Foster, Claire; Shreeve, David, 2007, *How Many Lightbulbs Does it Take to Change a Christian?: A Pocket Guide to Shrinking Your Ecological Footprint*, London: Church House Publishing.

Freire, Paulo, 2000 (1970), *Pedagogy of the Oppressed*, New York: Bloomsbury Academic.

Fromberg, Paul, 2017, *The Art of Transformation: Three Things Churches Do that Change Everything*, New York: Church Publishing.

Goodhart, David, 2017, *The Road to Somewhere: The Populist Revolt and the Future of Politics*, London: C. Hurst & Co.

Greenough, Chris, 2019, *Queer Theologies: The Basics*, London: Routledge.

Gustine, Adam L., 2019, *Becoming a Just Church: Cultivating Communities of God's Shalom*, Downers Grove, IL: IVP.

Gutiérrez, Gustavo, 1973, *A Theology of Liberation*, London: SCM Press.

Haidt, Jonathan, 2013, *The Righteous Mind: Why Good People Are Divided by Politics and Religion*, London: Penguin.

Hall, Stuart; Massey, Doreen; Rustin, Michael, 2015, *After Neoliberalism? The Kilburn Manifesto*, London: Lawrence and Wishart.

Han, Hahrie, 2014, *How Organizations Develop Activists: Civic Associations and Leadership in the 21st Century*, Oxford: Oxford University Press.

Havel, Vaclav, 1990, *Letters to Olga: June 1979 to September 1982*, London: Faber & Faber.

Higgins, Gregory C., 2009, *Wrestling with the Questions: An Introduction to Contemporary Theologies*, Minneapolis, MN: Fortress Press.

Hodgson, Phyllis (ed.), 1944, *The Cloud of Unknowing and Book of Privy Counseling*, Oxford: Early English Text Society.

Holmes, Lucy-Anne, 2015, *How to Start a Revolution*, London: Transworld.

Hope, Anne; Timmel, Sally, 1967, *Training for Transformation: A Handbook for Community Workers*, Harare: Mambo Press.

Houston, Fleur, 2015, *You Shall Love the Stranger as Yourself: Biblical Challenges in the Contemporary World*, London: Routledge.

Howson, Chris, 2011, *A Just Church: 21st Century Liberation Theology in Action*, London: Continuum.

Huxley, Justine Afra, 2019, *Generation Y, Spirituality and Social Change*, London: Jessica Kingsley.

Jones, James, 2003, *Jesus and the Earth*, London: SPCK.

Julian of Norwich, 2015, *Revelations of Divine Love*, Oxford: Oxford University Press.

Kabat-Zinn, John, 2013, *Full Catastrophe Living*, London: Piatkus.

Kelly, Kevin, 1992, *New Directions in Moral Theology*, London: Geoffrey Chapman.

King, David; Walker, Gabrielle, 2009, *The Hot Topic: How to Tackle Global Warming and Still Keep the Lights On*, London: Bloomsbury.

King Jr, Martin Luther, 2001, *Strength to Love*, Minneapolis, MN: Fortress Press.

Laird, Martin, 2006, *Into the Silent Land*, London: Darton, Longman and Todd.

Lane, Chris, 2017, *Ordinary Miracles: Mess, Meals and Meeting Jesus in Unexpected Places*, Watford: Instant Apostle.

Longacre, Doris Janzen, 2010, *Living More With Less* (30th Anniversary edition), Harrisonburg, VA: Herald Press.

Martin, Jim, 2012, *The Just Church: Becoming a Risk-taking, Justice-seeking, Disciple-making Congregation*, Carol Stream, IL: Tyndale House.

Mau, Bruce, 2004, *Massive Change*, London: Phaidon Press.

McGarvey, Darren, 2018, *Poverty Safari: Understanding the Anger of Britain's Underclass*, London: Picador.

MacLeod, J., 1993, *Community Organising: A Practical and Theological Evaluation*, London: Christian Action.

Morisy, Ann, 1997, *Beyond the Good Samaritan: Community Ministry and Mission*, London: Continuum.

——, 2004, *Journeying Out*, London: Bloomsbury.

——, 2011, *Borrowing from the Future: A Faith-based Approach to Intergenerational Equity*, London: Continuum.

Nouwen, Henri, 1996, *Reaching Out*, London: Fount.

Oakley, Nigel, 2007, *Engaging Politics? The Tensions of Christian Political Involvement*, Milton Keynes: Paternoster.

Ozanne, Jayne, 2016, *Journeys in Grace and Truth: Revisiting Scripture and Sexuality*, London: Ekklesia.

Palmer, G. E. H; Sheerard, P.; Ware, Kallistos (eds), 1979, *The Philokalia the Complete Text* (4 volumes), London: Faber & Faber.

Pearce, Nick; Paxton, Will, 2005, *Social Justice: Building a Fairer Britain*, London: Politico's Publishing.

Peterson, Jordan B., 2018, *12 Rules for Life: An Antidote to Chaos*, London: Penguin Random House UK.

Pickett, Kate; Wilkinson, Richard, 2010, *The Spirit Level: Why Equality is Better for Everyone*, London: Penguin.

Pliny the Elder, *Natural History*, translated by Harris Rackham, Loeb, 1950, Book XIX, Chapter LIV.

Pope Francis, 2013, *Evangelii Gaudium: The Joy of the Gospel*, London: The Incorporated Catholic Truth Society.

——, 2018, *Gaudete et Exsultate: On the Call to Holiness in Today's World*, London: The Incorporated Catholic Truth Society.

Pope Paul VI, 1975, *Evangelii Nuntiandi: On Evangelization in the Modern World*, London: The Incorporated Catholic Truth Society.

Popovic, Srdja; Millar, Matthew, 2015, *Blueprint for Revolution: how to use rice pudding, Lego men, and other non-violent techniques to galvanise communities, overthrow dictators, or simply change the world*, London: Scribe.

Porrit, Jonathan, 2013, *The World We Made: Alex McKay's Story from 2050*, London: Phaidon.

Pye, Ken, 2019, *Two Triangles: Liverpool, Slavery and the Church*, Diocese of Liverpool and USPG.

Rawls, John, 2001, *Justice as Fairness: A Restatement*, Cambridge, MA: Harvard University Press.

Ricketts, Aidan, 2012, *The Activists' Handbook: A Step-by-step Guide to Participatory Democracy*, London: Zed Books.

Ritchie, Angus, 2019, *People of Power: How Community Organising Recalls the Church to the Vision of the Gospel*, London: Centre for Theology and Community.

——, 2019, *Inclusive Populism: Creating Citizens in the Global Age* (Contending Modernities), London: University of Notre Dame Press.

Ritchie, Angus; Hackwood, Paul, 2014, *Just Love: Personal and Social Transformation in Christ*, Watford: Instant Apostle.

Rohr, Richard, 2014, *A Lever and a Place to Stand: The Contemplative Stance, the Active Prayer*, Mahwah, NJ: Paulist Press.

——, 2019, *The Universal Christ: How a Forgotten Reality Can Change Everything We See, Hope For and Believe*, London: SPCK.

Russell, Hilary, 2015, *A Faithful Presence: Working Together for the Common Good*, London: SCM Press.

Sagovsky, Nicholas; McGrail, Peter, 2015, *Together for the Common Good: Towards a National Conversation*, London: SCM Press.

Sainsbury, Roger, 1970, *From a Mersey Wall*, London: Scripture Union.

Schluter, Michael; Ashcroft, John, 2005, *Jubilee Manifesto: A Framework, Agenda and Strategy for Christian Social Reform*, Leicester: IVP.

Scott, Ruth, 2014, *The Power of Imperfection. Living Creatively With Human Complexity*, London: SPCK.

Segalov, Michael, 2018, *Resist! How to be an Activist in the Age of Defiance*, London: Laurence King.

Shaw, Randy, 1996, *The Activist's Handbook: A Primer*, London: University of California Press.

Sheppard, David, 1974, *Built as a City: God and the Urban World Today*, 2nd edn 1975, London: Hodder & Stoughton.

——, 1983, *Bias to the Poor*, London: Hodder & Stoughton.

——, 1984, *The Other Britain*, Northampton: Belmont Press.

Sheppard, David; Worlock, Derek, 1988, *Better Together*, London: Hodder & Stoughton.

Shukla, Nikesh, 2017, *The Good Immigrant*, London: Unbound.

Smith, Austin, 1983, *Passion for the Inner City*, London: Sheed & Ward.

——, 1990, *Journeying with God: Paradigms of Power and Powerlessness*, London: Sheed & Ward.

——, 2010, *Mersey Vespers: Reflections of a Priest and Poet*, Stowmarket: Kevin Mayhew.

Snyder, Susanna; Ralston, Joshua; Brazal, Agnes M., 2015, *Church in an Age of Global Migration: Pathways for Ecumenical and Interreligious Dialogue*, London: Palgrave Macmillan.

Solnit, Rebecca, 2016, *Hope in the Dark: Untold Histories, Wild Possibilities*, Edinburgh: Canongate.

Spencer, Nick, 2016, *Doing Good: A Future for Christianity in the 21st Century*, London: Theos.

Stanley, Bruce, 2013, *Forest Church: A Field Guide to Nature Connection for Groups and Individuals*, Powys: Mystic Church Press.

Stormzy, 2018, *Rise Up: The #merky Story So Far*, London, #Merky Books.

Stuart, Tristram, 2009, *Waste: Uncovering the Global Food Scandal*, London: Penguin.

Summers, Rachel, 2017, *Wild Lent*, Stowmarket: Kevin Mayhew.

——, 2018, *Wild Advent*, Stowmarket: Kevin Mayhew.

——, 2019, *Wild Worship*, Stowmarket: Kevin Mayhew.

Thorne, Brian, 2003, *Infinitely Beloved: The Challenge of Divine Intimacy*, London: Darton, Longman and Todd.

Threlfall-Holmes, Miranda, 2012, *The Essential History of Christianity*, London: SPCK.

Tutu, Desmond; Tutu, Mpho, 2014, *The Book of Forgiving*, London: Collins.

Tyler, Peter, 2018, *Christian Mindfulness*, London: SCM Press.

Varoufakis, Yannis, 2017, *Talking to My Daughter About the Economy: A Brief History of Capitalism*, London: Bodley Head.

Valerio, Ruth, 2008, *L is for Lifestyle Paperback: Christian Living That Doesn't Cost the Earth*, London: IVP.

Viola, Frank; Demuth, Mary, 2015, *The Day I Met Jesus: The Revealing Diaries of Five Women from the Gospels*, Grand Rapids, MI: Baker Books.

Waring, Marilyn, 1988, *If Women Counted: A New Feminist Economics*, New York: HarperCollins.

Welby, Justin, 2016, *Dethroning Mammon: Making Money Serve Grace*, London: Bloomsbury Continuum.

Wells, Samuel, 2015, *A Nazareth Manifesto*, Chichester: Wiley.

Wells, Samuel; Coakley, Sarah, 2008, *Praying for England: Priestly Presence in Contemporary Culture*, London: Continuum.

Wells, Samuel; Rook, Russell; Barclay, David, 2017, *For Good: The Church and the Future of Welfare*, Norwich: Canterbury Press.

Williams, Rowan, 2016, *On Augustine*, London: Bloomsbury.

Winstanley, Gerrard; Benn, Tony, 2011, *A Common Treasury*, London: Verso Books.

Witherington, Ben, 2001, *The Gospel of Mark: A Socio-rhetorical Commentary*, Grand Rapids, MI: Eerdmans.

Wright, Tom, 2001, *Mark for Everyone*, London: SPCK.

——, 2001, *Luke for Everyone*, 2nd edn 2004, co-published in London: SPCK; Louisville, KY: Westminster John Knox Press.

——, 2002, *John for Everyone Part 1*, 2nd edn 2004, co-published in London: SPCK; Louisville, KY: Westminster John Knox Press.

——, 2002, *John for Everyone Part 2*, 2nd edn 2004, co-published in London: SPCK; Louisville, KY: Westminster John Knox Press.

——, 2002, *Matthew for Everyone Part 1*, 2nd edn 2004, co-published in London: SPCK; Louisville, KY: Westminster John Knox Press.

——, 2002, *Matthew for Everyone Part 2*, 2nd edn 2004, co-published in London: SPCK; Louisville, KY: Westminster John Knox Press.

——, 2008, *Acts for Everyone Part 1*, London: SPCK.

——, 2008, *Acts for Everyone Part 2*, London: SPCK.

Yoder, John Howard, 1972, *The Politics of Jesus*, 2nd edn 1994, Grand Rapids, MI: Eerdmans.

Reports

Faith in the City: A Call for Action by Church and Nation: Report of the Archbishop of Canterbury's Commission on Urban Priority Areas, 1985.

Biographies

Annie Merry is originally from Suffolk. Her passions include growing food and being in nature, learning, music, people, social justice and human rights, reading and comedy – she has a strong spiritual connection to the earth. Annie has had a varied working life including hairdressing, catering, holistic drug, alcohol and sexual health, youth homelessness and waste management.

Spending time at a desert reclamation centre in Andalucia in her mid-twenties facilitated Annie's interest in human impact on the environment and climate change. She has a BA Hons in Peace Studies specializing in Conflict Resolution and Post Graduate (ILM) in Leadership for Sustainable Communities.

Annie has led Faiths4Change since its inception in 2004. In 2015 she was surprised (and pleased) to be awarded the Liverpool Echo Environment Award: Environmental Champion for outstanding contributions to improving the environment and health and well-being on Merseyside.

Revd Canon Dr Angus Ritchie has ministered in inner-city churches involved in community organizing since 1998, playing a leading role in successful campaigns for the Living Wage, affordable housing and a cap on interest rates. He is the Director of the Ecumenical Centre for Theology and

Community in east London. His latest book, *Inclusive Populism: Creating Citizens in the Global Age*, was published by the University of Notre Dame Press in September 2019.

Jenny Sinclair is founder Director of Together for the Common Good (T4CG), a charity helping people across the churches to strengthen the bonds of social trust. As a national volunteer-driven organization, T4CG equips and enables people to develop and practise the Common Good through training and resources. The work calls people to fulfil their vocational responsibility by putting Common Good principles into practice and by working with others of different opinions and backgrounds in shared purpose. T4CG's journey has been Spirit-led, and draws from across the Christian traditions, in particular Catholic Social Teaching. Its inspiration is rooted in the partnership between Jenny's father, Bishop David Sheppard, and Archbishop Derek Worlock in Liverpool a generation ago. Prior to 2011, Jenny was a graphic designer, screenprint artist and serial volunteer. Jenny was received into the Catholic Church in 1988, lives in London and is married with two adult sons.

Nadine Daniel was born and educated in Liverpool. She practised at the Criminal Bar for 25 years, and then as Project Coordinator for both the Anglican and Roman Catholic Cathedrals' Community Outreach Project, Hope+, an interdenominational and multi-faith response to all those in need in the city, especially those who came via the refugee crisis. Currently she is the National Refugee Welcome Coordinator, Church of England Archbishops' Council, in which role she advises the Archbishops' Council on the development of refugee policy for the Church of England. She also advises the 26 bishops who are The Lords Spiritual in Parliament on issues of forced migration and related legislation. She is responsible for the Church of England's role as a Principal Sponsor of the UK Government's Community Sponsorship Scheme.

Revd Bonnie Evans-Hills is an Anglican priest and acts as coordinator for the UK Coalition, working with the UN Office for Genocide Prevention, religious leaders and actors, focusing on transforming attitudes to refugees, migration, radicalization and hate crime in order to avert future atrocities. She has considerable experience in interreligious dialogue, peace-building and community development – working with the World Council of Churches, the Anglican Communion and the Church of England, among others. Bonnie is co-author, with Michael Rusk, of *Engaging Islam from a Christian Perspective*, published by Peter Lang, and has contributed to other publications.

Jane and Henry Corbett met when they were both doing a year as volunteers at Shrewsbury House in Everton, Liverpool in 1975–6. Jane then trained at Guy's Hospital, London and Henry at Wycliffe Hall, Oxford, before Henry returned to Everton as curate at St Peter's Church with Shrewsbury House in 1978. In 1979 they were married and have lived in Everton ever since, first in a tower block, then on the edge of the Radcliffe estate and from 1987 in St Peter's Vicarage.

Henry has been Area Dean for Liverpool North, is the chaplain to Everton FC's training ground, and is the vicar of St Peter's and St John Chrysostom's, Everton, and warden of Shrewsbury House. He has a first-class degree in theology.

Jane had been involved as a local activist for over 20 years before becoming Councillor for Everton ward in 2002; she was made Assistant Mayor for Fairness and Tackling Poverty in 2018, and has a Masters in Urban Regeneration.

They have three children, Emma, Sarah and Tom.

Revd Canon Dr Ellen Loudon is the Canon Chancellor of Liverpool Cathedral and Director of Social Justice for the Diocese of Liverpool. She is the Liverpool City Region Metro Mayoral advisor for the Voluntary and Community Sector and chair of the VS6, which represents the Voluntary, Community, Faith and Social Economy (VCFSE) in the region. She sits on the Diocese of Liverpool Bishop's Oversight team and serves as the Bishop's Chaplain for Social Justice. She is a trustee of a number of charities: Micah Liverpool, Together Liverpool and the Diocesan Council of Social Aid.

Ellen has a PhD in Music Hall, an MA in Pop Music, BA in Drama and BA in Theology. Before she was ordained she worked in the theatre and was a Senior Lecturer in Drama. Apart from work, she shares life with her husband Mark, a number of grown-up children who wish to remain anonymous and two dogs that don't care if she tells you that their names are Holly and Jacob. Mark and Ellen have a show on an internet radio station called 'In the Pop Kitchen' that is recorded in their actual kitchen.

Kieran Bohan is originally from London, now living in Liverpool. He trained for the Roman Catholic priesthood in his twenties, but chose not to be ordained. He is now a lay member of the leadership team at St Bride's CofE Church in Toxteth. In May 2012 he and Warren Hartley celebrated the first civil partnership to be registered in a place of worship in the UK. In March 2019 Kieran was commissioned by the Archdeacon of Liverpool as a Missional Leader with responsibility for outreach and pastoral care for the LGBT+ community, and training around gender and sexuality issues for faith communities, in the Diocese of Liverpool. He coordinates Open Table, a network of ecumenical worship communities for LGBTQIA+ Christians and all who seek an inclusive church. He is also part-time chaplain for a regional Christian charity supporting vulnerable adults.

Warren Hartley was born in Sydney, Australia, and grew up in a diverse range of churches, from High Church Anglican to Charismatic Pentecostal, before lapsing into angry atheism in his early twenties. Eight years later he experienced a spiritual awakening, which drew him back into exploring Christian faith. He followed a lifelong dream to come to the UK in 2006. Faith deepened, then love blossomed when he met Kieran in 2007 and they made Liverpool their home. Warren works for the Anglican Diocese of Liverpool, and volunteers as the LGBTQIA+ Ministry Facilitator at St Bride's Church Liverpool, co-leading the Open Table Liverpool community. When the vicar who set it up left, Warren was asked if he would open up the church and make tea – hospitality has been at the heart of Open Table ever since. In his spare time he'll be found either in the garden or sitting with knitting.

Dr Naomi Maynard is a Senior Qualitative Researcher at the Church Army. Her recent projects have focused on social action, discipleship and church growth. Previously, Naomi worked as a research and evaluation consultant, specializing in questions of faith, social justice and poverty alleviation. Naomi's doctorate examined youth participation in the UK, and she has published academic articles on youth activism and citizenship. Alongside her role at the Church Army, Naomi is a Project Development Worker for Together Liverpool. She lives in Liverpool with her husband and their sons Harvey and Donachie.

Dr Heather Buckingham is Head of Church Engagement at the Trussell Trust. She was previously Director of Research and Policy at the Church Urban Fund. Heather is a Fellow of the Edward Cadbury Centre for the Public Understanding of Religion and has worked as a Research Fellow at the University of Birmingham and the University of Southampton. Her PhD in Sociology and Social Policy explored the role of ethos in strategic decision-making and in day-to-day practices among faith-based and secular voluntary organizations working with homeless people.

Jessamin Birdsall Saunders is Head of Research and Evaluation at the Church Urban Fund and a PhD Candidate in Sociology and Social Policy at Princeton University. She is passionate about the intersections of theology, sociology and social justice. Jessamin has worked in the fields of community development and research in diverse contexts across Asia, Africa, North America, the South Pacific and the UK. Her research interests include inequality, migration, race and ethnicity, social capital, and religion. Jessamin is an active member of her local church community and believes in the power of the Christian gospel to catalyse personal and social transformation.

Church Land Programme Collective was initiated in 1996 as a joint project between the Association for Rural Advancement (AFRA) and the Pietermaritzburg Agency for Christian Social Awareness (PACSA), in response to the land reform process taking place in South Africa. It was established as an independent organization in 1997 and initially focused on church-owned land, while also challenging the Church to engage in the national land question and work for a just and sustainable agrarian transformation.

The Church Land Programme works to affirm, learn from and journey with those who are systematically excluded and impoverished in their struggles related to land and justice. CLP supports people's struggles for freedom and to regain their collective power. CLP works with people through a process of animation.

The collective is led by Graham Philpott and includes David Ntseng, Nomusa Sokhela, Zodwa Nsibande, Skhumbuzo Zuma, Zonke Sithole, Cindy Dennis and Phiwa Khumalo.

Father Richard Peers is Director of Education for the Diocese of Liverpool and Chief Executive of the diocesan Multi-Academy Trust. An Anglican priest, he has combined ordained life with full-time work in primary and secondary schools, including classroom teaching, chaplaincy, deputy headship and executive headship of both primary and secondary schools. Richard has been a practitioner and teacher of mindfulness to adults and children for over 30 years. An experienced Spiritual Director, he works with individuals and communities seeking to deepen their relationship with God and to grow in holiness. Richard is a founder and first leader of the Sodality of Mary, an international community of Anglican priests.

Revd Canon Malcolm Rogers is The Bishop of Liverpool's Canon for Reconciliation and also Vicar of St Gabriel's Church, Huyton Quarry, a post he has held for 20 years. Mal is a trustee of the Anthony Walker Foundation and in 2016 he received an MBE in the Queen's Birthday Honours List for his community cohesion work locally and internationally. In 2012 Mal helped set up the Triangle of Hope an international reconciliation project engaging young people from Africa, Liverpool and the United States. At Easter 2019, it was announced that Malcolm had been awarded a Senior Fellowship at his alma mater, Liverpool Hope University. In June 2019 he led a trip to Ghana, West Africa, involving 30 young people from around the Triangle of Hope. He firmly believes that education is the key to breaking down barriers, a work which, he contends, is needed more than ever before.

12 RULES FOR CHRISTIAN ACTIVISTS

Ann Morisy is an independent community theologian who lives in Streatham, south London, although you may be suspicious of her accent, which is more Bootle than Streatham! Ann is an internationally acclaimed lecturer whose presentations are down-to-earth but informed by scholarship as well as engaging and light-hearted. She has authored a number of well-regarded books on social action and the distinctive contribution that churches can make. Her 2011 book *Borrowing from the Future* addresses the issue of intergenerational fairness, calling on 'baby boomers' to play a pivotal part in attending to the well-being of the younger generation.

Acknowledgement of Sources